The Language of War

The INTERTEXT series has been specifically designed to meet the needs of contemporary English Language Studies. *Working with Texts: A core introduction to language analysis* (second edition, 2001) is the foundation text, which is complemented by a range of 'satellite' titles. These provide students with hands-on practical experience of textual analysis through special topics, and can be used individually or in conjunction with *Working with Texts*.

The Language of War:

◎ explores how military discourse has entered mainstream language use

◎ focuses on how language is used to construct opposing sides during armed conflict

◎ analyses the interaction between verbal and visual language in military propaganda

◎ compares and contrasts media coverage of war with the language of official reports

◎ draws on an eclectic range of military and non-military texts from a wide variety of sources

Steve Thorne studied as a mature student at the University of Birmingham and was awarded a Ph.D. in English in 2003. He currently works as an Essential Skills Team Leader at Birmingham Rathbone as well as a Visiting Lecturer at the University of Birmingham and an Associate Lecturer at the Open University, and has published widely in the field of attitudes towards Birmingham English.

The Intertext series

The Routledge INTERTEXT series aims to develop readers' understanding of how texts work. It does this by showing some of the designs and patterns in the language from which they are made, by placing texts within the contexts in which they occur, and by exploring relationships between them.

The series consists of a foundation text, *Working with Texts: A core introduction to language analysis*, which looks at language aspects essential for the analysis of texts, and a range of satellite texts. These apply aspects of language to a particular topic area in more detail. They complement the core text and can also be used alone, providing the user has the foundation skills furnished by the core text.

Benefits of using this series:

◎ **Multi-disciplinary** – provides a foundation for the analysis of texts, supporting students who want to achieve a detailed focus on language.

◎ **Accessible** – no previous knowledge of language analysis is assumed, just an interest in language use.

◎ **Student-friendly** – contains activities relating to texts studied, commentaries after activities, highlighted key terms, suggestions for further reading and an index of terms.

◎ **Interactive** – offers a range of task-based activities for both class use and self-study.

◎ **Tried and tested** – written by a team of respected teachers and practitioners whose ideas and activities have been trialled independently.

The series editors:

Adrian Beard was until recently Head of English at Gosforth High School, and now works at the University of Newcastle upon Tyne. He is a Chief Examiner for AS and A Level English Literature. He has written and lectured extensively on the subjects of literature and language. His publications include *Texts and Contexts* (Routledge).

Angela Goddard is Head of Programme for Language and Human Communication at the University College of York St John, and is Chair of Examiners for A Level English Language. Her publications include *Researching Language* (second edition, Heinemann, 2000).

Core textbook:

Working with Texts: A core introduction to language analysis
(second edition, 2001)
Ronald Carter, Angela Goddard, Danuta Reah, Keith Sanger and
Maggie Bowring

Satellite titles:

The Language of Advertising: Written texts
(second edition, 2002)
Angela Goddard

Language Change
Adrian Beard

The Language of Children
Julia Gillen

The Language of Comics
Mario Saraceni

The Language of Conversation
Francesca Pridham

The Language of Drama
Keith Sanger

The Language of Fiction
Keith Sanger

Language and Gender
Angela Goddard and Lindsey Meân
Patterson

The Language of Humour
Alison Ross

*The Language of ICT: Information and
communication technology*
Tim Shortis

The Language of Magazines
Linda McLoughlin

The Language of Newspapers
(second edition, 2002)
Danuta Reah

The Language of Poetry
John McRae

The Language of Politics
Adrian Beard

Language and Region
Joan C. Beal

The Language of Science
Carol Reeves

The Language of Speech and Writing
Sandra Cornbleet and Ronald Carter

The Language of Sport
Adrian Beard

The Language of Television
Jill Marshall and Angela Werndly

The Language of Websites
Mark Boardman

The Language of Work
Almut Koester

The Language
of War

 Steve Thorne

Routledge
Taylor & Francis Group

LONDON AND NEW YORK

First published 2006
by Routledge
2 Park Square, Milton Park, Abingdon, Oxon OX14 4RN

Simultaneously published in the USA and Canada
by Routledge
270 Madison Ave, New York, NY 10016

Routledge is an imprint of the Taylor & Francis Group

Typeset in Stone Sans/Stone Serif by
Florence Production Ltd, Stoodleigh, Devon
Printed and bound in Great Britain by
TJ International Ltd, Padstow, Cornwall

British Library Cataloguing in Publication Data
A catalogue record for this book is available from the British
Library

Library of Congress Cataloging in Publication Data
Thorne, Steve, 1967–
    The language of war/Steve Thorne
        p. cm. – (Intertext)
    Includes bibliographical references
    1. English language – Discourse analysis.   2. Military art
    and science – English-speaking countries – Terminology.
    3. Soldiers – English-speaking countries – Language.
    4. Military art and science – Terminology.   5. Soldiers –
    Language.   6. War – Terminology.   I. Title.   II. Series:
    Intertext (London, England)
    PE1422.T54 2006
    355.001'4 – dc22   2005026117

ISBN10: 0–415–35867–1 (hbk)
ISBN10: 0–415–35868–X (pbk)

ISBN13: 9–78–0–415–35867–5 (hbk)
ISBN13: 9–78–0–415–35868–2 (pbk)

contents

acknowledgements

Grateful acknowledgement is made to the following for permission to reproduce material in this book: Phil Hilton (2004) 'Who's the best?', *Nuts*. Copyright © 2004 IPC Syndication; Lorrayne Anthony (2004) 'The battle for beauty', *Lifewise Living*. Copyright © 2004 The Canadian Press; Dale Ritterbusch (1989) 'Search and destroy'. Copyright © 1989 Texas Tech University Press; Ministry of Defence (2003) 'Force level adjustments', www.operations.mod.uk/telic/statement_sofs_30april.htm; The White House (2001) 'Today We Mourned, Tomorrow We Work', www.whitehouse.gov/news/releases/2001/09/20010916–2.html; Imperial War Museum (2005) 'The Hun and the Home', 'Red Cross or Iron Cross', 'BRITONS', 'I WANT YOU FOR U.S. ARMY'. Copyright © 2005 Imperial War Museum; Unjustmedia (2005) 'Airdrop propaganda leaflet', www.the unjustmedia.com; Ministry of Defence (2005) 'JOIN THE ELITE'. Copyright © 2005 Ministry of Defence; *Daily Mirror* (2004) 'HIS COUNTRY NEEDS YOU'. Copyright © 2004 Mirror Group Newspapers; Ministry of Defence (2005) 'The Campaign', www.mod.uk/publications/iraq_lessons/chapter3.htm; EA Games (2002) 'You don't play, you volunteer'. Copyright © 2002 EA Games; America's Army (2005) 'Special Forces Hospital', www.americasarmy.com/intel/map_sfhospital.php.

Every effort has been made to contact copyright owners, but if any have been inadvertently overlooked, the publishers will be pleased to make the necessary arrangements at the earliest available opportunity.

introduction

In 1973, the National Council of Teachers of English (NCTE) formed a Committee on Public Doublespeak in order to expose the way in which language was increasingly being used to deceive by those in power. According to the NCTE website (www.ncte.org/about/gov/commit/106 942.htm), the function of the Committee is:

> To create a series of concrete classroom exercises (lesson plans, discussion outlines) calculated to focus student attention on particular uses of language that the Committee is prepared to call irresponsible; and alert the profession generally to the forces that in the Committee's judgment are misusing the language: government and its military personnel, industry and its advertisers, educators, you and me.

William Lutz, the Committee Chair, defines doublespeak as:

> language that pretends to communicate, but really doesn't. It is language which makes the bad seem good, the negative seem positive, the unpleasant appear attractive, or at least tolerable. Doublespeak is language which avoids or shifts responsibility, language which is at variance with its real or purported meaning. It is language which conceals or prevents thought. Rather than extending thought, doublespeak limits it.
>
> (1994: 318)

The word 'doublespeak' is often incorrectly attributed to George Orwell's *1984* (1949). Orwell did, however, use the term 'newspeak' in *1984* to refer to deliberately ambiguous or contradictory language and in his earlier essay, 'Politics and the English Language' (1946), he criticises the English of his day, citing examples of 'dying metaphors', 'verbal false limbs', 'pretentious diction' and 'meaningless words', all of which, he states, contribute to fuzzy ideas and a lack of logical thinking. Towards the end of this essay, having argued his case, Orwell muses:

> Political language – and with variations this is true of all political parties, from Conservatives to Anarchists – is designed to make lies

sound truthful and murder respectable, and to give an appearance of solidity to pure wind.

Orwell appears to be implying, in other words, that the language used by those in power – whether they be politicians, government officials, military personnel or religious leaders – is by its very nature dishonest, deceitful and manipulative.

The NCTE Doublespeak Award, established in 1974, is presented annually by the Committee to those who have used language that is deliberately deceptive, evasive, euphemistic, vague, confusing or self-centred. The recipient of the first Award was Colonel David H. E. Opfer, the United States Air Force Press Officer in Cambodia. After a US bombing raid, he allegedly told reporters: 'You always write it's bombing, bombing, bombing. It's not bombing! It's air support!' Many other recipients of the Award have also had close links with the military. In 1977, for example, the Pentagon and US Energy Research and Development Administration were presented with the Award for describing the neutron bomb as 'an efficient nuclear weapon that eliminates an enemy with a minimum degree of damage to friendly territory'. In 1983, the Award was presented to US President Ronald Reagan for naming the MX Intercontinental Ballistic Missile 'Peacekeeper' and for proclaiming that 'a vote against MX production today is a vote against arms control tomorrow'. In 1984, the US State Department received the Award for announcing that it would no longer use the word 'killing' in official reports on the status of human rights in other countries, but would replace it with the phrase 'unlawful or arbitrary deprivation of life'; in 1991 the US Department of Defense received the Award for referring to bombing attacks as 'efforts' and warplanes as 'weapons systems' or 'force packages'; and US President George W. Bush was presented with the award in 2003 and 2004 for coining such phrases as 'weapons of mass destruction-related program activities'.

In view of this, it seems surprising that not a single book has been written on the subject of military doublespeak. Although a handful of books have been written on the subject of doublespeak in general – William Lutz's *Doublespeak: From 'Revenue Enhancement' to 'Terminal Living': How government, business, advertisers, and others use language to deceive you* (1987), *The New Doublespeak* (1996) and *Doublespeak Defined: Cut through the bull**** and get the point* (1999) being perhaps the best examples – none has looked specifically at the language of war. The aim of the book you are about to read is to fill this void.

Fighting talk

THE MILITARISATION OF ENGLISH

Over hundreds of years, the English language has undergone a steady process of militarisation. Words and phrases of military origin have entered mainstream usage and become naturalised. As a result, we are rarely conscious of the fact that we are using military terminology in routine interaction. This has led to claims that the naturalisation of language better suited to war adversely affects the way we interact with others and renders us incapable of living peacefully. Throughout this book we will be examining the technical and non-technical use of military language as well as the effect that this has on English speakers. In order to denaturalise the language of war, we will begin with a discussion of militarisms in mainstream use.

The term **metaphor** will be used frequently in this unit. Unlike a **simile**, which compares two things by saying that one is like the other, a metaphor compares two things by saying that one is the other. For example, if we say that someone runs 'like lightning', we are using a simile to make an unrealistic comparison between the speed of the runner and the speed of lightning. We are also using a simile if we say that someone runs 'as quick as lightning'. If we say that someone is a 'lightning runner', on the other hand, we are using the word 'lightning' in a metaphorical rather than literal **sense** to describe the speed of the runner. English is rich in both similes and metaphors. One of the most common metaphors in English is 'time is money': This will *save* you a lot of *time* / Stop *wasting* my *time*. / She's living on *borrowed time*. / I've *invested* a lot of *time* in this. / It wasn't *worth* the *time* and effort. /

1

He's *lost* a lot of *time*. / You're *running* out of *time*. Time, of course, is not money, but by establishing this **analogy** in sentences such as those above, we suggest that time is valuable. Some metaphors are so common that we do not really see them as metaphors any more. Those that have become everyday or hackneyed expressions due to excessive use are known as **dead metaphors** or **clichés**.

The word 'war' can similarly be used in either a literal or metaphorical sense. If we say that two countries 'go to war', we are using war in the literal sense of an armed conflict between two opposing 'sides' (we will look in more detail at how language is used to legitimise, promote and justify these 'sides' in Unit three: Us and them). Although the sport of football also involves two sides, if we say that two football teams 'go to war', we are using war in a metaphorical sense. A football match is a sporting contest rather than an armed conflict and rarely results in the death of players, but war metaphors appear frequently in sports coverage.

In an interview prior to the 2003 World Cup, England rugby union coach Clive Woodward used metaphor to establish an analogy between the rugby field and the trenches of the First World War. Not only did he refer to the England management headquarters as 'the War Room', but he also spoke about the players being 'prepared to die for one another' and stated that 'there is not one man here that you would not want beside you in the trenches'. The football pitch is also likened to a battlefield on the front cover of the first edition of *Nuts*, a men's weekly magazine. This is achieved through the metaphorical use of the word 'war' to describe a competition between Thierry Henry and Ruud van Nistelrooy to become the season's top goalscorer: 'Now It's War! Thierry vs Ruud in the closest title race ever.' In the article entitled 'Who's the best?', van Nistelrooy is described as 'cool as a cucumber during the "Battle of Old Trafford" earlier this season'. This sentence contains both a simile and a metaphor. 'Cool as a cucumber' is a simile implying that van Nistelrooy was calm and imperturbable, and 'Battle of Old Trafford' is a metaphor implying that a match at Manchester United's home ground resembled armed combat rather than football.

Activity

1   Working in pairs or groups, if possible, see if you can find any other military metaphors in the third page of the *Nuts* article (see Text 1: Who's the Best?). What function do these metaphors serve?

2   Look through other examples of sports writing, preferably from different sources and covering a wide variety of sports. Highlight any military metaphors that you can find. Is the use of war metaphors restricted to the coverage of certain types of sport or indiscriminate?

SPORT RUUD VS THIERRY

WHO'S THE REAL LEADER?

THERE'S NOTHING like scoring the first goal of a match to settle the nerves and send your team on the way and here there's little to separate the Premiership's two leading marksmen. Six of Henry's 16 goals have been Arsenal's opener (38 per cent) while six of van Nistelrooy's 18 strikes have been United's first of the game (33 per cent). Surprisingly, the Frenchman has been the only name on the Arsenal score sheet just three times this season (against Portsmouth, Dynamo Kiev and Charlton) while his Old Trafford rival has been the only United player to find the back of the net on two occasions (against Charlton and Stuttgart). "I think that Henry adds more to Arsenal than van Nistelrooy does to Manchester United," Five Live's Mark Bright told *Nuts*. "If I had the money to buy just one, then I'd go for the Frenchman."
NUTS SAYS: Both central to their teams, but Henry edges this category.

"Lads, come and look at my Ruud puppet"

"Stop patting me on the head"

RAISING THE GAME

WHO'S THE DEADLIEST FINISHER?

VAN NISTELROOY enjoys the edge in terms of goals scored this season and he also has a better record than Henry in terms of accuracy and converting his chances. Overall, the deadly Dutchman is on target with 59 per cent of his efforts on goal and scores with 27 per cent of his attempts. In total, 52 per cent of Henry's shot are goal-bound and 13 per cent of his efforts find the back of the net. And the story is much the same whether you look at the stats based on home or away performances – van Nistelrooy still boasting a significantly better conversion rate on the road – 33 per cent to Henry's 13 per cent. The Frenchman, however, does have a significantly higher number of attempts at goal overall – firing off 126 efforts this season compared to van Nistelrooy's more modest 68. "Ruud's more of a striker and he'll always outscore Henry," TalkSport's Alan Brazil told *Nuts*. "He's a better finisher and his placement inside the 18-yard box is much more canny."
NUTS SAYS: If we're talking about clinical finishing then it's got to be the Dutchman.

SHOOT TO KILL

"Oh bugger, he's going the right way..."

WHO IS MORE OF A TEAM PLAYER?

HENRY IS WIDELY regarded as the more effective team player and the stats back up the argument. The Highbury striker is credited with ten goal assists for the Gunners in contrast to van Nistelrooy's three and he has weighed in with 124 crosses for team-mates compared to the Dutchman's meagre 20. He also leads in the number of passes attempted, with 705 to van Nistelrooy's 560. But the clincher is in Henry's overall contribution to the Gunners' attack – the Frenchman has played a part in 53 per cent of Arsenal's goals this term against the Dutchman's 40 per cent for United. "There is something very singular and ruthless about van Nistelrooy," says former England boss Terry Venables. "Henry has greater complexity and awareness as a team player."
NUTS SAYS: Henry the undisputed winner.

"Who stole my beach ball?"

WHO GETS STUCK IN THE MOST?

STRIKERS AREN'T known for their love of tackling but even superstars like Henry and van Nistelrooy are prepared to get their knees dirty from time to time. The Frenchman boasts an impressive 69 per cent success rate when he goes in for the ball, compared to van Nistelrooy's 64 per cent. But the Dutchman can still lay claim to the bragging rights as he has put his foot in 42 times so far this season – ten more times than his French rival.
NUTS SAYS: Van Nistelrooy by a nose.

"Doin' the Lambeth walk, oi!"

NOW YOU DECIDE... The Nuts office was reduced to a war zone by the Henry versus van Nistelrooy debate, so we're asking you to decide for us. The Highbury hitman or the Dutch destroyer? Log on to our website at www.nutsmag.co.uk to vote.

ALL STATS ARE PREMIERSHIP AND CHAMPIONS LEAGUE ONLY UP TO 12 JANUARY

opta index

3

Commentary

Both van Nistelrooy and Henry are described as 'the Premiership's two leading marksmen' in the first text box. The second text box is entitled 'WHO'S THE DEADLIEST FINISHER?', and van Nistelrooy is not only described as 'the deadly Dutchman' but also as 'on target'. When discussing attempts at goal, Henry is described as 'firing off 126 efforts this season compared to van Nistelrooy's more modest 68', and the photograph in the bottom left-hand corner of the article is entitled 'SHOOT TO KILL'. A reference is made to the Gunners' (a nickname for Arsenal, Henry's team) 'attack' in the third text box. As well as describing an editorial discussion of the merits and demerits of the two players as a 'war zone', the 'Now you decide. . .' text box in the bottom right-hand corner of the article also describes Henry as 'the Highbury hitman' and van Nistelrooy as 'the Dutch destroyer'.

'Marksmen', 'deadliest', 'deadly', 'on target', 'firing off', 'shoot to kill', 'attack', 'war zone', 'hitman' and 'destroyer' are words and phrases originally used by the military, and all of these are used in a metaphorical sense in the article to reinforce the idea that football is war. (Words such as 'versus', 'ruthless' and 'rival', furthermore, are thrown in to intensify the notion that the two players are locked in mortal combat with each other.) When comparing the media coverage of other sports, you may have noticed that the use of military metaphors such as these is not indiscriminate. Although war metaphors are just as likely to occur in the coverage of team sports such as football and rugby as they are in sports involving individual competitors such as boxing and tennis, they are more likely to occur in commentaries on high-contact sports such as boxing rather than non-contact sports such as golf.

WAR ALL THE TIME

Military metaphors are by no means limited to the language of sport. They can appear anywhere and in a wide variety of forms. Politicians, for example, often resort to the metaphorical use of military terminology:

> The government has consistently got away with intellectually *indefensible* policies.

> Democratic presidential candidate Al Sharpton *launched a blistering attack* on Howard Dean yesterday.

The continuing *fallout* over the Hutton report proves that judges and politics don't mix.

Gregory pointed out how Bush had received a lot of political *flak* from conservatives, mainly talk show host Rush Limbaugh, over yesterday's reports.

'Fallout', in its literal sense, is the precipitation of radioactive particles from a nuclear explosion, but it is used here in its metaphorical sense to mean an adverse and unwanted side-effect or repercussion. 'Flak', an abbreviation of the German 'Fliegerabwehrkanone', meaning 'aviator defence gun', was a term originally adopted by the military for the fire from anti-aircraft guns, but here it is used metaphorically to mean strong criticism.

War metaphors like these are common in the world of commerce. The following, for example, was from a news item on the Sony website (sony.gamerweb.com/news/0502/004.asp, link no longer available):

SCEA *dropped a bombshell* on gamers today, as it lowered the price on many Playstation hardware items, including the main console to $199. The price cut may be in response to rumors that Microsoft would cut the price of the Xbox at its press conference on Monday May 21. The strongest rumor had Microsoft leading the *price cut wars*, but now Sony has *drawn first blood*. It remains to be seen if Microsoft and Nintendo will follow suit.

(We will look at the language of video games in Unit six: Virtual war.) We may also use military metaphors to discuss health:

Of course, there is the more traditional use of *combating* illness with prescribed antibiotics.

A type of seaweed could be more effective at *fighting* flu than conventional drugs, according to scientists in Japan.

The *arsenal* for *battling* breast cancer has grown considerably over the past few years.

After she is *blitzed* with cancer-killing medication, her own stem cells are returned to her body.

'Blitz', an abbreviation of the German 'Blitzkrieg', from 'Blitz' (lightning) + 'Krieg' (war), was a term originally used by the military for a rapid and violent military attack with intensive aerial bombardment, but here it is used as a **verb** meaning to subject something or someone to an intense burst of energy or activity. Even beauty treatments can be described in terms of war.

Activity

Text 2: The Battle for Beauty is an internet article by Lorrayne Anthony on a new type of cosmetic surgery.

1   Read through the article and identify as many military metaphors as possible.

2   What analogy does the author draw between beauty and war?

Text 2: The Battle for Beauty

THE BATTLE FOR BEAUTY

Heat from radio frequencies used in latest weapon against aging skin

by Lorrayne Anthony

THE EXPENSE, THE PAIN AND the recovery time are just a few of the reasons why some people shy away from getting a facelift. But what if you could turn back the clock without going under the knife?

With promises of a tighter, more youthful appearance, the latest weapon in age-defying – known as Thermage, ThermaLift or ThermaCool – is being used by plastic surgeons and dermatologists across the country.

Cleared for use earlier this year by Health Canada, the technique uses heat from radio frequencies to reconfigure the collagen that lies under the skin in order to tighten or lift. It can be used on the forehead, cheeks and jawline.

While not meant to replace the traditional nip and tuck, Thermage can be used as a precursor to a facelift.

Such a device has been 'a missing weapon in the arsenal of anti-aging procedures,' said Dr. Stephen Mulholland, surgical director of SpaMedica, a cosmetic surgery

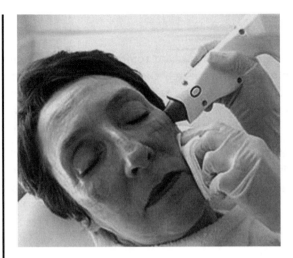

The Thermage procedure is demonstrated on patient Carol Wood in Toronto Wednesday May 21, 2003. The non-surgical procedure uses radio frequency to target the deep layers of the skin and cause tissue tightening, thus diminishing wrinkles, fine lines and sagging.

and laser dermatology clinic in Toronto. 'It's not going to last forever, but if you have a focused, pre-emptive strike approach to your face you can often delay surgery indefinitely.'

Dr. Julie Khanna, a plastic surgeon at the Institute of Cosmetic and Laser Surgery in Oakville, Ont., agrees.

'This can buy you a little time,' said Khanna, who would sometimes see a patient come in to talk about getting a facelift. She would look at the patient and think a facelift wasn't needed, but instead the person might benefit from non-surgical procedures. This is where Thermage comes in.

'Let's do the Thermage to lift things a little, Botox to erase any lines and (intense light therapy) to help even out skin colouring,' said Khanna. 'And then in a few years we can talk facelift.'

Thermage is aimed at people 35–55 who don't want any recovery time. As Khanna's colleague at the institute, Dr. Sheetal Sapra, said: 'This is perfect for people – men – who are wimps' and don't want to go under the knife.

(See the commentary on p. 91.)

Activity

1   Make a list of around ten words that are commonly associated with war. Input these into an internet search engine and find an example of each of your military words being used in a literal and metaphorical sense (you may find it useful to draw up a table with two columns, one for the word in its literal sense, the other in its metaphorical sense).

2   Assign the war metaphors to a specific **genre** of writing or speech, such as sports, politics, business, health, advertising, everyday conversation, etc. Are there any genres of writing in which war metaphors would seem out of place?

3   Is the use of metaphors such as these innocuous?

Commentary

As well as 'battle', 'shoot', 'kill', 'attack', 'target', 'combat', 'weapon' and 'arsenal', which have already been discussed, the following words appeared most frequently in lists compiled by students at the University of Birmingham:

gun, rifle, cannon, soldier, bomb, army, sword, armour, troops, battle-ground

Among those that occurred less frequently were 'bullet', 'enemy', 'shield', 'conflict', 'shotgun', 'salvo', 'flank', 'pressgang', 'spearhead', 'snipe', 'barrage', 'calibre', 'shellshocked', 'ballistic', 'retreat' and 'conquest'. All of these can be used both literally and metaphorically. Typical examples of the ten most common words taken from a range of internet sources include:

gun
Literal use: Thirteen people, including several Shiites, were *gun*ned down in the northeastern town of Hungu last week following Nawaz's execution.
Metaphorical use: President Arroyo is the most experienced among the crop of candidates *gun*ning for the presidency in May.

rifle
Literal use: Despite advances in machine gun, mortar and grenade technology, all remained relatively unwieldy and cumbersome in comparison to the *rifle*, which remained the most crucial, ever-present infantry weapon throughout the First World War.

Metaphorical use: Ahmed Hassan received a low cross from the right wing, he got the ball under control despite the heavy marking on him and managed to *rifle* a shot at goal.

cannon

Literal use: Robert P. Parrott is known to many Civil War artillery researchers and collectors for his inventions of the projectile and *cannon* which bear his name.

Metaphorical use: It was all-action football in the early stages and Brazil almost pulled a goal back on seven minutes when Igor turned smartly in the area, and fired in a shot that *cannon*ed back off the near post when he should have scored.

soldier

Literal use: This database compiles information on Polish *soldier*s who died during the Second World War and were buried in different cemeteries in France.

Metaphorical use: That these firms had *soldier*ed on in the face of these difficulties was probably because they felt that Zimbabwe's crisis could be overcome sooner rather than later.

bomb

Literal use: President George Bush *bomb*ed Baghdad and invaded Somalia in the two months between his electoral defeat in November 1992 and Clinton's inauguration in January.

Metaphorical use: On 17 January the Office of Fair Trading (OFT) dropped a *bomb*shell on the community pharmacy sector.

army

Literal use: New German *Army* Chief of Staff Paul von Hindenburg consequently despatched August von Mackensen to assist the Bulgarians with their own military preparations later that year.

Metaphorical use: An *army* of news reporters descended on the village of Iron River, Michigan, to squash a 'whiskey rebellion' that had captured headlines throughout the country.

sword

Literal use: The concept of Kendo is to discipline the human character through the application of the principles of the Japanese *sword*.

Metaphorical use: The head of one of the country's highest profile dotcoms fell on his *sword* today, but he may have created even more problems for Telstra in doing so.

armour

Literal use: This fifteenth century suit of *armour* comes with etched engrav-
ings on the breastplate, helmet, and gauntlets.

Metaphorical use: In 2002 a small chink in his *armour* showed when Santiago
Botero beat him soundly over the 55km stage 9 TT course in Lorient.

troops

Literal use: Washington had also seen the busy movements of the British
troops in the hills and their impressive baggage train.

Metaphorical use: Sydney's leading trainer Gai Waterhouse marshalled her
troops with military precision as bands of jockeys and horses darted in
and out of the mounting enclosure.

battleground

Literal use: This was the first war where the number of mutilated soldiers that
survived their *battleground* wounds outnumbered the number of the
casualties.

Metaphorical use: Can your religious beliefs make it across our intellectual
battleground?

'Pressgang', originally a **collective noun** for a group of sailors who
forcibly recruited men into the navy, is now commonly used metaphorically
as a verb meaning to force anyone to do something against their will: 'We
were grabbed almost as soon as we arrived and pressganged into moving
tables.' It is possible to sharpen a spearhead and spearhead a campaign:
'Priests spearhead campaign to make celibacy optional'; use a shield to fend
off accusations as well as blows: 'He has also shielded himself in a timely
fashion from possible accusations of nepotism'; and snipe with words as
well as a gun: 'She's tired of Musgrove and Republican challenger Haley
Barbour sniping at each other.'

'Salvo' can be used literally as a simultaneous discharge of artillery, or
metaphorically as a burst of repeated criticisms: 'Railtrack chairman John
Robinson has delivered a vicious assault on the Government, launching a
salvo of criticism over its handling of the company's demise.' We may refer
to sexual partners as 'conquests', go 'ballistic' when angry, or feel 'shellshocked' when under stress. We may also be subjected to a 'barrage' of
abuse rather than artillery shells, and use 'calibre' to refer metaphorically to
a person's character rather than the diameter of a bore of a gun: 'It enables
you to email details of your graduate vacancies, work experience opportun-
ities and careers events directly to thousands of high-calibre students,
postgraduates and, from Autumn 2002, graduates.'

There are few genres of writing or speech in which **conceptual
metaphors** such as these would seem out of place. This is because the

language of war, to adopt another widely used metaphor, is inextricably woven into the fabric of English; so much so that the original military sense of some words and phrases has faded from the collective consciousness. For example, 'harbinger', from the Old English 'heriberga', was originally a military term for a person who travelled before an army to find accommodation for the troops. Now it is used in a more generalised sense to mean a precursor or forerunner of any kind. A 'blockbuster' was originally a large bomb used to demolish a number of buildings simultaneously. Now it is mainly used in reference to a commercially successful film.

Activity

1   Research the **etymology** of the following words and phrases: alarm, ambulance, bachelor, berserk, caddie/caddy, canteen, crusade, field day, freelance, garret, gauntlet, gremlin, jeep, kamikaze, loophole, magazine, marathon, picket, pioneer, slogan, snorkel.

2   Were you surprised to learn that they all started out as military terms?

(There is no commentary for this activity.)

It is impossible to know for sure how the use of war metaphors became so widespread. One likely explanation for the militarisation of English is that it was initiated by soldiers returning from war and applying military terminology to non-military contexts. The mainstream use of language formerly restricted to specific occupations is by no means unusual. For example, there are many maritime metaphors in English that were originally introduced by sailors returning from sea:

> HRDC employees had received oral directives to review their files, fill in the blanks, and backdate documents if necessary so that everything looked *shipshape*.

> The government seems to have *battened down the hatches* for the dreaded eventuality of the current variant of bird flu coming to Singapore.

> Meanwhile, entrepreneur Rod Hemphill has *taken the helm* of Sotheby's International Realty's Hout Bay, Llandudno and Camps Bay franchises.

11

She drank it down in a few short gulps and *keeled over*.

Foreign Minister Alexander Downer *delivered a broadside* yesterday against the Zimbabwe Government over the handling of its political crisis.

In fact, once you get to *know the ropes*, you will begin to use it on automatic pilot, without even thinking about it.

If one is willing to believe the happy talk from music business executives, the *tide has finally turned* against file sharing.

What is unusual, however, is the sheer number of military metaphors in common use. Analysis of this kind inevitably uncovers a wide variety of structural military metaphors: sport is war, love is war, politics is war, religion is war, business is war, advertising is war, medical progress is war, etc. We battle with the elements, combat fatigue, fight the flab, defend our own points of view while attacking those of others on a daily basis and life itself becomes a war.

It might be argued that metaphorical expressions, whatever their origin, are harmless and help enrich the English language, but one of the most commonly heard criticisms of military metaphors is that they trivialise war and cheapen the memory of those who fought and/or died in battle. In the following extract from an article that first appeared in the *USA Today* newspaper, journalist and author Robert Lipsyte condemns the cynical use of military metaphors in sports coverage as well as the use of sporting metaphors in war coverage as repulsive and even dangerous:

> Ever since 9/11, the customary practice of describing sports events in the language of war has seemed particularly repulsive. Nevertheless, sportscasters still have teams 'blitzing' and 'throwing bombs', and games still end in 'sudden death'. Just part of the hype, I thought – obnoxious but probably harmless. But when I heard a broadcaster say Gen. Tommy Franks had 'called an audible at the line of scrimmage' in Iraq, the mingling of sports and war language suddenly seemed surreal, even dangerous. How could the deadly decision to switch from 'shock and awe' to the 'surgical decapitation' of Saddam Hussein be depicted in the breezy jock jargon of a quarterback changing an offensive play at the last minute? Was I being a little too sensitive here? 'Not at all,' said retired lieutenant general Bradley Hosmer, who served in Vietnam. 'There's something of a play-by-play quality to the coverage that runs the risk of trivializing the horrors of war. Go ask the families who have lost soldiers if they were playing a game.'

Another criticism of the proliferation of militaristic expressions is that it subconsciously shapes the way we think, affects our behaviour and limits our ability to live our lives in peaceful terms. In *The Argument Culture* (1998), for example, Deborah Tannen suggests that: 'Military metaphors train us to think about – and see – everything in terms of fighting, conflict, and war. This perspective then limits our imaginations when we consider what we can do about situations we would like to understand or change.' The theory that the language we use to some extent influences the way we think is known as linguistic determinism and has generally been split into two main types: 'strong' determinism and 'weak' determinism. Strong determinism holds that language completely determines thought, whereas weak determinism holds that language merely affects thought. Although few linguists today would support the theory that language has the power to completely shape the way we view the world, the theory that language has the capacity to influence our world-view is widely accepted.

When discussing the 'Metaphor System Used to Justify War in the Gulf' in a paper presented on 30 January 1991 at the University of California, the linguist George Lakoff proclaimed that metaphors can kill:

> The discourse over whether to go to war in the gulf was a panorama of metaphor. Secretary of State Baker saw Saddam Hussein as 'sitting on our economic lifeline.' President Bush portrayed him as having a 'stranglehold' on our economy. General Schwarzkopf characterized the occupation of Kuwait as a 'rape' that was ongoing. The President said that the US was in the gulf to 'protect freedom, protect our future, and protect the innocent,' and that we had to 'push Saddam Hussein back.' Saddam Hussein was painted as a Hitler. It is vital, literally vital, to understand just what role metaphorical thought played in bringing us in this war.

In their book, *Language and Peace* (1999), Christina Schäffner and Anita Wenden assert that **structural metaphors** such as those listed above do not exist in a vacuum, but are related to one another and systematically organised at a higher, ideological level. Through the use of military metaphors, they point out, the language of sport, love, politics, religion, commerce, advertising, medicine and everyday conversation legitimises war as the natural and perhaps only effective way of solving problems, regulating relationships and settling inter-group conflict. They conclude that the language of journalists, sportsmen and women, politicians, religious leaders, health specialists, etc., not only legitimises war, but also

13

propagates war by unquestioningly promoting warlike values and attitudes, and justifies war by creating an 'us' (ally) and 'them' (enemy) that are essential to provoking and maintaining hostility. In other words, war metaphors are far from innocuous: they have become part of the belief system in English-speaking society, and as such colour the way we view the world and interact with others.

Extension

Find an example of written English that contains both structural and conceptual military metaphors.

1   Consider the ways in which these metaphors affect the discourse.

2   Is Deborah Tannen right to suggest that military metaphors are restrictive?

3   What evidence can you find to support the theory that language influences thought?

FURTHER READING

Lakoff, G. (2003) *Metaphors We Live By*. Chicago, IL: University of Chicago Press.

Verbal armoury

Discovery V8i, 1998, 3-door, LHD. 12,000 miles only. First Reg. May 1998 (KSA). Unreg. and unmodified for UK. White exterior, beige exterior. Air-con, central locking, stereo, electric windows and mirrors.

What type of text is this? You probably identified it immediately as a classified advertisement for a car, but what enabled you to do so? Was it the subject matter or use of language? Here are three other text types for you to identify:

Reduce heat and add Parmesan cheese. Heat and stir till fairly smooth. Stir in wine, parsley and water. Cook uncovered for 3 minutes or till slightly thickened. Serve sauce over hot cooked pasta. Garnish with fresh basil, if desired.

The ftp server on black can do automatic tar, compress and gzip. Appending '.tar' to the name of the directory will cause a 'get' command to tar the directory tree on the fly. Appending '.tarZ' to the name of a directory will cause a 'get' command to tar the directory tree on the fly and compress the result.

Your ruler Mercury forms a positive aspect to the moon, making today a good one for introspection. Thinking will get you everywhere today, but if you don't understand something, ask for assistance. We all need a bit of a helping hand sometimes.

The first text type is from a recipe, the second is from a computer manual and the third is from a horoscope. The subject matter and use of language in each instance enabled you to make fairly intuitive guesses as to where these texts are from. This is because language varies, not only according to the characteristics of the particular user (the source of **accents** and **dialects**), but also according to the characteristics of use (the source of **registers**).

The term 'register' is used by linguists to refer to a variety of language determined by topic, subject matter or activity, such as the register of classified car advertisements, the register of recipes, the register of computer manuals, the register of horoscopes, etc. This is usually a matter of vocabulary. Terms such as 'V8i', '3-door', 'LHD' and 'central locking', for example, are typically found in classified car advertisements. Some registers, however, have defining grammatical characteristics. Recipes, for example, characteristically contain verbs in the **imperative mood**, such as 'reduce', 'add', 'heat', 'stir', 'serve' and 'garnish' (see p. 15).

Registers are often subdivided into three domains: **field**, referring to the subject matter or activity type of the variety, such as cars, cookery, computers or star signs; **mode**, referring to the choice between spoken and written language as well as the choice of format; and **tenor**, referring to the kinds of social roles and/or relationships enacted in or by the variety, as shown by variations in formality. Field, mode and tenor, then, are different aspects of a text's context of use, and the type of field/mode/tenor determines the register.

Activity

Text 3: Search and Destroy was written by Dale Ritterbusch, who served with the US Army as an infantryman during the Vietnam War.

1   Comment on the use of language in the poem, paying particular attention to register, field, mode and tenor.

2   What sort of audience do you think this poem was intended for?

Text 3: Search and Destroy

Search and destroy

They came out of the hootch
with their hands up – surrendered –
and we found all that rice
and a couple of weapons. They
were tagged and it all seemed so easy –
too easy, and someone started to torch
the hootch and I stopped him – something
was funny. We checked the hootch
a couple times more; I had them probe it
like we were searching for mines and
a lucky poke with a knife
got us the entrance to a tunnel.
We didn't wait for any damn
tunnel clearers – we threw down
CS smoke and maybe two hundred
yards to our right two gooks popped up
and we got 'em running across the field,
nailed 'em before they hit the trees.
We went to the other hole and popped more
gas and smoke and a fragmentation grenade
and three gooks came out coughing, tears
and red smoke pouring out of their eyes and
nose. We thought there were more
so we threw in another grenade and one of the
dinks brought down his arms, maybe he started
to sneeze with all that crap running out of his face,
maybe he had a weapon concealed, I didn't know,
so I greased him. Wasn't much else I could do.
A sudden move like that.

Commentary

The poem is written in a military register, and the field is summed up in the title as a military 'search and destroy' operation. CS, a form of irritant gas that affects vision and respiration, is an **initialism** of Corson and Stoughton, who first synthesised O-chlorobenzylidene malonontrite in 1928. This is the only example of technical military language in the poem, but there is a considerable amount of military **slang**. 'Hootch', for example, was US Army slang for a civilian Vietnamese dwelling, and both 'gook' and 'dink' were derogatory terms used by US soldiers for Vietnamese civilians, Viet Cong (National Liberation Front) and/or NVA (North Vietnamese Army) soldiers. 'Tag' is slang for handcuff and 'torch' means burn. 'Nail' and 'grease' are used **dysphemistically** as verbs meaning 'kill' and are symptomatic of the bravado that characterises the tone throughout the poem.

Although the mode is obviously written, the poem has many of the characteristics of spoken language. There are a number of **colloquialisms**. 'Damn', for example, is used colloquially as an **adjective** in line 13, 'them' is abbreviated to 'em in lines 17 and 18, 'crap' is used in line 26 to refer to a discharge caused by the CS gas, and the **subject** of the second **clause** in line 28 is omitted: [There] wasn't much else I could do. **Sentence** structure, furthermore, is not particularly complex. Clauses in lines 4 to 7, for example, are bound together with a succession of **conjunctions**:

> They were tagged *and* it all seemed so easy – too easy, *and* someone started to torch the hootch *and* I stopped him.

There are few **subordinate clauses**, and this lack of structural complexity is a characteristic of spoken language. The tenor of the poem can therefore be described as relatively informal.

Vietnam war films such as *Apocalypse Now* (1979), *Platoon* (1986) and *Full Metal Jacket* (1987) have popularised US Army slang, but it is unlikely that many civilians would have understood the meaning of slang terms such as 'hootch', 'gook' and 'dink' when the poem was written. The poem relies heavily on assumed shared knowledge between the author and reader and can be interpreted in a number of ways. The use of language in the poem may symbolise the author's membership of a particular social group: US Vietnam War veterans. We could perhaps be even more specific and say that this social group includes US infantrymen or 'grunts' but excludes officers. If interpreted in this way, Ritterbusch appears to use military slang in order to signify his membership of this particular group, to communicate with those who shared the same or similar experiences, and to exclude those who did not. In doing so, he cements social bonds with fellow veterans and defines his own identity. On the other hand, Ritterbusch may be satirising the speaker's callous attitudes towards his victims rather than affirming solidarity with him.

Written ministerial statements are official documents produced by members of parliament. These are usually read out in the House of Commons and then published in Hansard – the printed reports of debates and committees in both houses of parliament. The register of Text 4: Force Level Adjustments, a *Written Ministerial Statement to the House of Commons by Secretary of State for Defence, Geoff Hoon (30 April 2003)* on force level adjustments in Iraq, is clearly military.

1   Discuss the field, mode and tenor of the statement and describe the ways in which the register differs from that of the poem above.

2   In *Standard English: What it isn't* (1999), Peter Trudgill notes:

   [it is] an interesting question as to how far technical registers have a technical function – that of, for example, providing well-defined unambiguous terms for dealing with particular topics – and how far they have the more particularly sociolinguistic function of symbolising a speaker or writer's membership of a particular group, and of, as it were, keeping outsiders out.

   In what way does Hoon's use of language symbolise his membership of a particular group?

3   Does Hoon assume any degree of prior knowledge of the subject he is discussing? If so, who is he attempting to exclude?

Text 4: Force Level Adjustments

Written Ministerial Statement to the House of Commons by Secretary of State for Defence, Geoff Hoon (30 April 2003)

In my written statement of 11th April, I said that we would continue to adjust our forces deployed to the Gulf region as appropriate, withdrawing units whose tasks are complete, and in due course replacing those whose tasks continue.

Decisive combat operations in Iraq are now complete, and coalition forces are increasingly focussing upon stabilisation tasks. It will therefore be possible to make further force level adjustments over the coming weeks while continuing to meet our responsibilities to the Iraqi people.

For maritime forces, the re-deployment of Royal Navy vessels has proceeded as planned. HMS *Ark Royal* has now left the Gulf region and is due to return to the UK in mid-May accompanied by the destroyer HMS *York* and RFA *Fort Victoria*. In addition, we now plan to withdraw the helicopter carrier, HMS *Ocean*, together with HMS *Edinburgh* and the Royal Fleet Auxiliaries *Fort Austin*, *Orangeleaf*, *Sir Bedivere* and *Sir Percivale*. The RFAs *Sir Galahad*, *Sir Tristram*, and *Bayleaf* are undertaking a rolling programme of maintenance in Singapore to allow them to return to the Gulf to continue to provide support to the humanitarian assistance effort. Further vessels will remain there for the time being to conduct mine clearance operations and force protection.

As the need for offensive air operations and close air support has significantly diminished, we can bring back further air assets. We have withdrawn around 45 aircraft from the Gulf region, both fixed and rotary wing, including Tornado F3 and GR4, Harrier GR7, Nimrod MR2, VC10 and E-3D aircraft as well as Chinook and Sea King helicopters. A further 26 helicopters will be withdrawn at the same time as HMS *Ocean*.

For land forces, conditions now allow for the return of a further 3,500 personnel to the UK. This will include 2nd Royal Tank Regiment and 1st Battalion The Royal Irish Regiment, with elements of 26 Regiment Royal Artillery, 38 Engineer Regiment and 1st Battalion The Light Infantry. It will also include a number of individuals who were attached to a wide variety of ground units and formations to perform specific augmenting roles. Returning forces are due a period of post-operational tour leave to which they are entitled, following which they will begin to prepare for training and then redeployment on other important operational taskings. In some cases, this will mean a return to Iraq to take part in continuing operations. In addition, we intend to withdraw 3 Commando Brigade Royal Marines, who were the first of the land formations to be deployed, during the course of May.

We will now begin to prepare 19 Mechanised Brigade to take over from forces previously involved in combat operations in Iraq, allowing us to meet the continuing task of providing a stabilisation force within the UK area of operations. We would expect them to start this new task in July, commencing preparations immediately.

In spite of these changes significant pressures remain on the Armed Forces if they are to meet the full range of their commitments. In order to meet our continuing obligations in Iraq, I have authorised the issuing of further call-out notices, against the Order made in January under section 54(1) of the Reserve Forces Act 1996, sufficient to generate up to 1,200 reservists. There will be a requirement to call out further reservists as the operation proceeds, and I will keep the House informed of our plans. In parallel, we will be starting to demobilise those Reserves who are returning home. In time, the overall numbers of Reserves required in Iraq will reduce significantly. I have also decided to extend the tour of the 1st Battalion The Duke of Wellington's Regiment, enabling them to continue in their key role of ensuring security in the region of Az Zubayr.

While details continue to be clarified, we envisage that by mid-May 25–30,000 UK Service personnel will remain deployed in the Gulf region, continuing to fulfil our responsibilities towards the Iraqi people. The planned replacement of forces is clear evidence of our commitment to them.

Our aim is to leave an Iraq that is confident, secure and fully integrated with the international community. The planning process to establish the precise level of the continuing UK presence needed to achieve this aim is a dynamic one, and is kept under review. We will also need to take account of the contributions of coalition partners. We will continue to withdraw assets and personnel from the region where possible, but we will maintain an appropriate military presence for as long as necessary.

(There is no commentary for this activity.)

MILITARY NAMING CONVENTIONS

You may have noticed that Hoon uses a number of technical military terms in his ministerial statement that would not be understood by civilians. Most of these are names. In this section we will look more closely at conventions used by the military to name weaponry, warships, attack aircraft, etc. We will look at why names such as Sir Bedivere, Sir Percivale, Sir Galahad and Sir Tristram are chosen for warships, why military aircraft are given names such as Harrier, Nimrod and Chinook, and why there are so many initialisms such as HMS, RFA, F3, GR4, GR7, MR2, VC10 and E-3D in military language.

Martin Montgomery, in his *An Introduction to Language and Society* (1995), stresses that nothing in language is impartial:

> In apprehending, comprehending and representing the world we inevitably draw upon linguistic formulations. One might say that because of this we always see it slightly askew. But it is not so much a question of bias that is at stake here. What it amounts to in fact is that there is no absolutely neutral and disinterested way of apprehending and representing the world. Language always helps to select, arrange, organize and evaluate experience, even when we are least conscious of it doing so. In this sense representation is always interested: the words chosen are selected from a determinate set for the situation at hand and have been previously shaped by the community, or by those parts of it, to which the speaker belongs.

Military terms such as the following, for example, may at first appear to be fairly disinterested lexical choices, but on closer analysis prove to be quite the opposite:

> blue on blue: the accidental death of allied soldiers;
>
> collateral damage: the accidental death of civilians;
>
> daisy cutter: the largest conventional bomb in existence;
>
> demographic targeting: the premeditated killing of civilians;
>
> export the risk: to shoot first and ask questions later;
>
> kinetic targeting: bombing;
>
> mop up: to finish off the last remnants of enemy resistance within a specified area;

mousehole: to blow a hole in the side of a building in order to gain entry;

smart bomb: a computer-guided or electronically controlled missile;

speed bump: anything that slows down the progress of war;

surgical strike: an attack aimed at destroying an individual target;

target servicing: subjecting a designated area to intense artillery bombardment;

transfer tube: a casket containing the dead body of a soldier.

Not only do these terms give a false sense of accuracy and sophistication, but they are also deliberately cryptic, abstruse, vague and highly evasive. The term 'blue on blue', for example, is derived from war games where allies are usually blue and enemies, in a hangover from the Cold War (see Unit three: Us and them), are red. It was first used in 2003 to describe the destruction of an RAF Tornado by a US Patriot missile. Used in this context, it appears to imply that war is just a game.

The term 'mop up' makes war sound like a domestic chore, and the terms 'daisy cutter', 'mousehole' and 'speed bump' are all used in a similarly **euphemistic** way by the military in an attempt to make the unpleasant sound more pleasant. The 15,000-pound 'daisy cutter' (or BLU-82) bomb was used by the US Air Force in Afghanistan as an anti-personnel weapon. These bombs explode a few feet above ground and obliterate anything within hundreds of yards. 'Mouseholing' is a technique used in urban warfare to avoid trip wires and booby traps at entrances to buildings by blasting holes in side walls with high explosives. It was used by Israeli troops in Palestine and resulted in numerous civilian deaths. The fighting at Basra and Umm Qasr during the war in Iraq were both referred to as 'speed bumps'. This seemingly innocent term makes the fierce resistance encountered by British and American troops sound insignificant.

'Kinetic targeting', 'smart bomb', 'surgical strike' and 'target servicing' make military operations and items of military hardware sound more precise than they actually are. 'Demographic targeting' and 'collateral damage', a term used in 1999 when US warplanes fired on a convoy of ethnic Albanians in Kosovo believing they were Serb forces, evade responsibility, as does 'export the risk', a euphemism first used by US troops serving in Iraq in reference to procedures at checkpoints for handling civilians suspected of being irregular forces or suicide bombers.

An analysis of military name changes can often be just as revealing as an analysis of naming conventions. After the First World War, for example, traumatised veterans were described as 'shellshocked'. This term vividly conveys the horrors of modern warfare. The term 'combat fatigue' was used to describe the same condition after the Second World War. Although this term acknowledges that combat was the cause of the trauma, it is less graphic. Traumatised Falklands War veterans were diagnosed as suffering from 'post-traumatic stress disorder', a term that seems completely disconnected from the horrors of war.

During the Vietnam War, the containers used to transport the dead bodies of soldiers home were referred to by the US military as 'body bags'. The Pentagon renamed them 'human remains pouches' during the 1991 Gulf War. During the war in Iraq in 2003, the Pentagon sanitised the name further by renaming them 'transfer tubes'. It is also worth noting that the US Department of Defense was formerly known as the Department of War.

Activity

1   Read the following list of names of British warships, both past and present, and add any more that spring to mind. (The initialism HMS stands for (His or) Her Majesty's Ship.)

HMS *Brazen*; HMS *Courageous*; HMS *Daring*; HMS *Fearless*;
HMS *Furious*; HMS *Gallant*; HMS *Hardy*; HMS *Hostile*;
HMS *Impulsive*; HMS *Indomitable*; HMS *Inflexible*; HMS *Invincible*;
HMS *Matchless*; HMS *Obdurate*; HMS *Relentless*; HMS *Savage*;
HMS *Taciturn*; HMS *Tenacious*; HMS *Undaunted*; HMS *Valiant*;
HMS *Vigilant*

2   In what way could it be said that these names are 'interested'?

3   Can you suggest any names that would appear unsuitable for a warship?

Commentary

All of these names are adjectives that conform to common patriarchal gender stereotypes. Stereotypes are socially shared opinions: generalised and simplified stock mental images or clichés that are seldom the end product of a careful assembly and balanced analysis of evidence, as has been shown by a number of psychological studies that reveal vast discrepancies between stereotypes and reality. Gender stereotypes occur when generic attributes or roles are applied to either gender. Adjectives such as 'gallant', 'fearless', 'taciturn' and 'tenacious' are more often used to describe male rather than female attributes. The feminine **pronouns** 'she' and 'her' are normally used in reference to ships (a tradition dating back hundreds of years, when female figureheads were mounted at the bow of sea-going vessels), but the warships above are thus gendered as masculine. Together the names of these warships build up a patriarchal notion of masculinity and what it is to be male: one of physical strength, uncommunicative stubbornness and an adherence to stereotypically masculine codes of bravery, gallantry and intrepidity.

You might also have added to the list names incorporating **nouns** rather than adjectives, such as HMS *Warrior* or HMS *Dreadnought* (meaning 'fear nothing'). Again, these have distinctly male as opposed to female **connotations**. A good way to find names that sound unsuitable for a warship is to find **antonyms** for those listed above:

> HMS *Bashful*; HMS *Soft*; HMS *Timid*; HMS *Fearful*; HMS *Calm*;
> HMS *Weak*; HMS *Feeble*; HMS *Friendly*; HMS *Cautious*;
> HMS *Compliant*; HMS *Docile*; HMS *Fragile/Vulnerable*; HMS *Inferior*;
> HMS *Tender*; HMS *Submissive*; HMS *Humane*; HMS *Talkative*;
> HMS *Pliant*; HMS *Timorous*; HMS *Shrinking*; HMS *Forgetful*

Together these build up a stereotypically male notion of femininity, and it is highly unlikely that the Royal Navy would ever seriously consider adopting them as names for warships. It is perhaps pertinent to note that military naming conventions are thus firmly at odds with the type of image that the armed forces currently attempt to portray in newspaper, magazine, radio and TV advertisements in their efforts to attract more female recruits. An analysis of military naming conventions reveals a firmly entrenched gender bias: one that suggests that feminine attributes have no worth during wartime and that war is most certainly no place for a woman.

Some military names are borrowed from folklore and superstition, hence Sir Bedivere, Sir Percivale, Sir Galahad and Sir Tristram (all characters from Arthurian legend), Dragon (a portable anti-tank weapon), Phoenix (a long-range air-to-air missile with electronic guidance), Genie (an air-to-air rocket with a nuclear warhead) and Sea Sprite (an anti-submarine helicopter). Some are biblical in origin. Nimrod (a maritime reconnaissance aircraft used by the RAF), for example, is named after a great grandson of Noah, the traditional founder of the ancient Babylonian dynasty and 'mighty hunter' (Genesis). Names such as these give the impression that a just or moral war is being waged whenever these weapons, warships or aircraft are used.

Other names are taken from classical mythology: Titan (a rocket-powered intercontinental ballistic missile with a nuclear warhead) is named after the original Greek gods who battled with the Olympians for supremacy; Poseidon (a submarine-launched missile) is named after the Greek god of the sea with a furious rage (Trident, another submarine-launched missile, is named after the three-pronged weapon carried by Poseidon); Hercules (a troop and cargo transport aircraft) is named after the Greek strongman and hero; Orion (a long-range anti-submarine aircraft) is named after the great hunter of Greek myth; and Vulcan (an army air defence artillery gun) is named after the Roman god of fire and metalworking who preceded Mars as god of war. It is no coincidence that these names were all originally associated with warlike and predominantly male deities with immense destructive power. They were specifically chosen to signify that these weapons and aircraft are all guided by a higher and much more powerful hand than that which created them.

A considerable number of weapons, warships and military aircraft are named after animals. Again, these are deceptive. There are missiles named Quail (an air-launched decoy carried by bombers), Condor (an air-to-surface missile), Hawk (a mobile surface-to-air missile), Falcon (an air-to-air guided missile), Shrike (an air-launched anti-radiation missile), Sparrow (an air-to-air solid propellant missile), Hound Dog (a jet-propelled air-to-surface missile) and Terrier (a surface-to-air missile with a rocket motor); aircraft named Tomcat (a long-range interceptor), Eagle (a supersonic fighter), Harrier (an attack aircraft designed to take off vertically) and Sea Cobra (a light attack helicopter); and warships and submarines named HMS *Antelope*, HMS *Gazelle*, HMS *Lion*, USS *Narwhal* and USS *Scorpion*. Although many of these animals are harmful, it could be argued that the use of names such as these anaesthetises civilians to the realities of modern warfare.

Names adopted by the US military typically tend to evoke a mythic ideal of the 'wild west': Chaparral (a short-range surface-to-air artillery system) is named after the dense tangled brushwood common in California; Bronco (an observation aircraft armed with machine guns) is named after a half-tamed horse; and Minuteman (an intercontinental ballistic missile) takes its name from American militiamen who fought during the War of Independence. Iroquois (a light, single-rotor helicopter armed with machine guns or rockets), Apache (an attack helicopter) and Chinook (a troop and cargo transport heli-copter) are names of native American tribes, and Tomahawk (a long-range cruise missile) is named after a native American war-axe.

Names such as Patriot (a mobile surface-to-air missile), Freedom Fighter (a supersonic fighter/bomber), Peacekeeper (an intercontinental ballistic mis-sile), Vigilante (a reconnaissance aircraft designed to operate from aircraft car-riers), Safeguard (a ballistic missile defence system) and Provider (an assault aircraft) deliberately and quite openly play on the jingoism, fears and insecurities of civilians, whereas others are much more euphemistic. For example, 'Little Boy' was the nickname of the atomic bomb dropped by the US on the Japanese city of Hiroshima on 6 August 1945, and 'Fat Man' was the nickname of the bomb dropped on Nagasaki three days later. Neither sounds like a weapon that killed hundreds of thousands of people. This is because both names obscure the true horror of atomic warfare by creating an illusory sense of benignancy and innocence. None of the names listed above are as innocuous as they appear at first glance, and analysing them in such a way reveals the interested character of linguistic representation.

Activity

Military **acronyms** such as AWOL (absent without leave) and initialisms such as OTT (over the top) and WMD (weapons of mass destruction) are now in common use. Here is a list of further acronyms and initialisms used by the military:

AO; AWACS; C&C; DADCAP; DEFCON; DMZ; E&E; EPW; ERW; FIBUA; GI; GSW; HARM; HQ; HVT; ICBM; KIA; LGB; LOCAP; LP; LZ; MAD; MBT; MFC; MIA; MIRV; MOAB; MOPP; MOUT; MP; PDF; POW; PTSD; RFA; RPG; R&R; SAM; SLBM; SNAFU; SSE; SSK; TLAM; TPFDL; TWS; UXB; WIA; WP

1   Do you know what any of these acronyms or initialisms stand for?

2   Can you add any more acronyms or initialisms to this list?

3   It might be said that military acronyms and initialisms such as these serve a practical purpose in that they shorten lengthy and rather cumbersome terms when time is at a premium, but can you think of any other reason why acronyms and initialisms are so common in military language?

(There is no commentary for this activity.)

Extension

1 Input 'weapon specifications' into an internet search engine and visit one of the many websites run by weapons manufacturers or suppliers. Make a list of the names of weapons you find. What percentage of these names contain either acronyms, initialisms or numbers?

2 The following are the names of guns listed on the Modern Firearms and Ammunition website (world.guns.ru/main-e.htm):

> FN Browning HP-DA; SIG-Sauer P245; Walther PPK; HK P2000; IM Metal HS 2000; FN FNP-9/PRO-9; SA Vz.58; APS 95; FN F2000; IMBEL MD-2; AK47 AKM; INSAS; AEK-971; CIS SAR-80; CETME mod. LC; SIG 510/Stgw.57; XM29 OICW; Steyr IWS 2000; KSVK 12.7; Savage 10FP; RAI/RAP model 300; HK CAWS; TOZ-194; Vector SS-77; M249 SAW; Browning BAR M1918; Kalashnikov RPK-74

Do you know what any of these acronyms, initialisms or numbers stand for?

3 In *Language in Popular Fiction* (1990), Walter Nash discusses the 'buzz' of technological specification in the macho man's **lexicon**. How might this account for the abundance of acronyms, initialisms and numbers used in weapon specifications?

FURTHER READING

Reinberg, L. (1991) *In the Field: The language of the Vietnam war.* New York: Oxford.

three

Us and them

Language can be used to provoke hostilities between nations in much the same way as it can between social groups and individuals. Clashes between rival football supporters, drunken bar room brawls and fights in school playgrounds inevitably begin with name-calling, verbal abuse and/or threats, and international disputes are no different. As noted in Unit one: Fighting talk, all wars require an 'us' (friend) and a 'them' (foe), and language plays a pivotal role in the creation of these identities. This unit will look at the ways in which opposing 'sides' before, during and after armed conflict are constructed, legitimised and maintained through language use. It will look at the ways in which language is used to construct identity and difference, and will focus, in particular, on how a sense of otherness is created linguistically.

In *Orientalism* (1979), Edward Said questions a wide variety of assumptions made about the East (the Orient) by the West (the Occident). 'The Orient', Said suggests, is a sweeping generalisation created by the West: one which stereotypes Eastern civilisation as inferior and alien (i.e. 'other') in relation to Western civilisation. *Orientalism* has been heavily criticised as anti-Western, but, in the afterword to the 1995 edition of his book, Said dismisses this claim by pointing out that neither East nor West corresponds with any sort of stable reality:

the development and maintenance of every culture require the existence of another and competing *alter ego*. The construction of identity – for identity, whether of Orient or Occident, France or Britain, while obviously a repository of distinct collective experiences, *is* finally a construction – involves establishing opposites and 'others' whose actuality is always subject to the continuous interpretation and re-interpretation of their differences from 'us'. Each age and society creates its 'Others'. Far from a static thing then, identity of self or of 'other' is a much worked-over historical, social, intellectual, and political process that takes place as a contest involving individuals and institutions in all societies.

In short, we define ourselves (us) in relation to others (them) and we do this by constructing competing identities for both sides through language use.

The simplest and perhaps most common way of establishing opposites and 'others' is through the use of personal pronouns. Pronouns are used in place of nouns or **noun phrases** to refer to people or things without actually naming them. The table below shows how pronouns differ depending upon **person** (first, second or third), **gender** (male, female or neuter) and whether they are used in the **singular** or **plural** form.

	Nominative (subject)	Accusative (object)	Genitive (possessive)	
Singular			*(1 adjective)*	*(2 pronoun)*
First person	I	me	my	mine
Second person	you	you	your	yours
Third person	he	him	his	his
	she	her	her	hers
	it	it	its	its
Plural				
First person	we	us	our	ours
Second person	you	you	your	yours
Third person	they	them	their	theirs

Pronouns also differ depending upon whether they are used in the **nominative** (subject), **accusative** (object) or **genitive** (possessive) **case**. But pronouns are not merely a way of expressing person, gender, number or case. They also play a key role in the construction of identity and difference. When we use the plural third person pronoun in its nominative (they), accusative (them) or genitive (their/theirs) case, for example, we either consciously or subconsciously evoke a sense of otherness. By contrasting a 'them' with an 'us', we are effectively saying that they are unlike us: that they are different or perhaps inferior in some way. They may, of course, be unlike us because they are separated from us by distance or time. But what about if they share the same space and time with us? What function would the use of pronouns such as 'we', 'us', 'they' and 'them' serve in this instance?

In most pronoun studies, as Mühlhäusler and Harré point out in *Pronouns and People: The linguistic construction of social and personal identity* (1990), the distinction between inclusive and exclusive is used as a label in subcategorising **pronominal systems**:

> The distinction is based on whether the addressee is excluded or included in the referential sphere of forms such as *we*. . . . Language-specific conventions for including or excluding secondary persons with primary pronouns are to be seen as an important indicator for self- and other-centred pronoun systems.

Inclusive 'we' is often used by authors. In the paragraph above, for example, I use the plural first person pronoun in its nominative case three times in order to include myself, the reader and all English speakers in the referential sphere:

> When <u>we</u> use the plural third person pronoun in its nominative (they), accusative (them) or genitive (their/theirs) case, for example, <u>we</u> either consciously or subconsciously evoke a sense of otherness. By contrasting a 'them' with an 'us', <u>we</u> are effectively saying that they are unlike us: that they are different or perhaps inferior in some way.

In doing so, I simultaneously exclude all non-English speakers from the referential sphere. This establishes a common bond between myself, the reader and all English speakers, and identifies non-English speakers as 'other'.

Inclusive 'we' can also be used as a **rhetorical device** to manipulate emotions. When Winston Churchill famously declared in his wartime speech of 4 June 1940:

> We shall go on to the end, we shall fight in France, we shall fight on the seas and oceans, we shall fight with growing confidence and growing strength in the air, we shall defend our island, whatever

the cost may be, we shall fight on the beaches, we shall fight on the landing grounds, we shall fight in the fields and in the streets, we shall fight in the hills; we shall never surrender,

he was including all Britons in the referential sphere. Classical rhetoric recognised persuasion as one of the main aims of communication (the other two being education and entertainment), and few would doubt the persuasiveness of Churchill's words, which were not only successful in helping to galvanise the British people at a time when morale was worryingly low, but also in forewarning the other (i.e. the Axis powers) of British determination to resist invasion.

Activity

Text 5: Today We Mourned, Tomorrow We Work, is a transcript of remarks made by US President George W. Bush shortly after the attacks on the Pentagon and World Trade Center on 11 September 2001. The full text was posted on the White House website as an official news release on 16 September 2001.

1   Comment on Bush's use of plural first and third person pronouns throughout the text.

2   Who is being included and who is being excluded when Bush uses plural first person pronouns?

3   How does the use of the word 'crusade' affect your answer to the question above?

Text 5: Today We Mourned, Tomorrow We Work

Remarks by the President Upon Arrival
The South Lawn

THE PRESIDENT: Today, millions of Americans mourned and prayed, and tomorrow we go back to work. Today, people from all walks of life gave thanks for the heroes; they mourn the dead; they ask for God's good graces on the families who mourn, and tomorrow the good people of America go back to their shops, their fields, American factories, and go back to work. Our nation was horrified, but it's not going to be terrorized. We're a great nation. We're a nation of resolve. We're a nation that can't be cowed by evil-doers. I've got great faith in the American people. If the American people had seen what I had seen in New York City, you'd have great faith, too. You'd have faith in the hard work of the rescuers; you'd have great faith because of the desire for people to do what's right for America; you'd have great faith because of the compassion and love that our fellow Americans are showing each other in times of need. I also have faith in our military. And we have got a job to do – just like the farmers and ranchers and business owners and factory workers have a job to do. My administration has a job to do, and we're going to do it. We will rid the world of the evil-doers. We will call together freedom loving people to fight terrorism. And on on this day of – on the Lord's Day, I say to my fellow Americans, thank you for your prayers, thank you for your compassion, thank you for your love for one another. And tomorrow when you get back to work, work hard like you always have. But we've been warned. We've been warned there are evil people in this world. We've been warned so vividly – and we'll be alert. Your government is alert. The governors and mayors are alert that evil folks still lurk out there. As I said yesterday, people have declared war on America, and they have made a terrible mistake, because this is a fabulous country. Our economy will come back. We'll still be the best farmers and ranchers in the world. We're still the most innovative entrepreneurs in the world. On this day of faith, I've never had more faith in America than I have right now.

Q: Mr. President, are you worried this crisis might send us into a recession?

THE PRESIDENT: David, I understand that there are some businesses that hurt as a result of this crisis. Obviously, New York City hurts. Congress acted quickly. We worked together, the White House and the Congress, to pass a significant supplemental. A lot of that money was dedicated to New York, New Jersey and Connecticut, as it should be. People will be amazed at how quickly we rebuild New York; how quickly people come together to really wipe away the rubble and show the world that we're still the strongest nation in the world. But I have great faith in the resiliency of the economy. And no question about it, this incident affected our economy, but the markets open tomorrow, people go back to work and we'll show the world.

Q: Mr. President, do you believe Osama bin Laden's denial that he had anything to do with this?

THE PRESIDENT: No question he is the prime suspect. No question about that.

Q: Mr. President, can you describe your conversation with the President of Pakistan and the specific comments he made to you? And, in addition to that, do you see other – you've asked Saudi Arabia to help out, other countries?

THE PRESIDENT: John, I will – obviously, I made a call to the leader of Pakistan. We had a very good, open conversation. And there is no question that he wants to cooperate with the United States. I'm not at liberty to detail specifically

33

what we have asked him to do. In the course of this conduct of this war against terrorism, I'll be asked a lot, and members of my administration will be asked a lot of questions about our strategies and tactics. And in order to protect the lives of people that will be involved in different operations, I'm not at liberty to talk about it and I won't talk about it. But I can tell you that the response from Pakistan; Prime Minister Vajpayee today, of India, Saudi Arabia, has been very positive and very straightforward. They know what my intentions are. They know my intentions are to find those who did this, find those who encouraged them, find them who house them, find those who comfort them, and bring them to justice. I made that very clear. There is no doubt in anybody's mind with whom I've had a conversation about the intent of the United States. I gave them ample opportunity to say they were uncomfortable with our goal. And the leaders you've asked about have said they were comfortable. They said, we understand, Mr. President, and we're with you.

Q: Mr. President, the Attorney General is going to ask for enhanced law enforcement authority to surveil and – things to disrupt terrorism that might be planned here in the United States. What will that mean for the rights of Americans? What will that mean –

THE PRESIDENT: Terry, I ask you to talk to the Attorney General about that subject. He'll be prepared to talk about it publicly at some point in time. But what he is doing is, he's reflecting what I said earlier in my statement, that we're facing a new kind of enemy, somebody so barbaric that they would fly airplanes into buildings full of innocent people. And, therefore, we have to be on alert in America. We're a nation of law, a nation of civil rights. We're also a nation under attack. And the Attorney General will address that in a way that I think the American people will understand. We need to go back to work tomorrow and we will. But we need to be alert to the fact that these evil-doers still exist. We haven't seen this kind of barbarism in a long period of time. No one could have conceivably imagined suicide bombers burrowing into our society and then emerging all in the same day to fly their aircraft – fly US aircraft into buildings full of innocent people – and show no remorse. This is a new kind of – a new kind of evil. And we understand. And the American people are beginning to understand. This crusade, this war on terrorism is going to take a while. And the American people must be patient. I'm going to be patient. But I can assure the American people I am determined, I'm not going to be distracted, I will keep my focus to make sure that not only are these brought to justice, but anybody who's been associated will be brought to justice. Those who harbor terrorists will be brought to justice. It is time for us to win the first war of the 21st century decisively, so that our children and our grandchildren can live peacefully into the 21st century.

Commentary

The plural first person pronoun in the nominative case is used 31 times in the text – much more than the plural first person pronoun in the accusative case, which is used twice, the plural first person pronoun in the genitive case (adjective), which is used ten times, and the plural first person pronoun in the genitive case (pronoun), which is not used at all. Bush first uses the plural first person pronoun in the nominative case in his opening line and appears to be including all Americans (i.e. US citizens) in the referential sphere: 'Today, millions of Americans mourned and prayed, and tomorrow we go back to work.' A common bond is thus immediately established between Bush and his US audience. This bond is strengthened when Bush uses the plural first person pronoun in the genitive case (adjective) to refer to 'our nation' and when he uses the plural first person pronoun in the nominative case a further three times: 'We're a great nation. We're a nation of resolve. We're a nation that can't be cowed by evil-doers.'

However, the referential sphere does not remain constant throughout the text. A few lines further on, for example, Bush appears to be including himself and the US military in the referential sphere: 'I also have faith in our military. And we have got a job to do', but shortly afterwards only Bush and the Bush administration are included in the referential sphere: 'My administration has a job to do, and we're going to do it. We will rid the world of the evil-doers. We will call together freedom loving people to fight terrorism.' Bush then includes himself and the US Congress (an elected group of politicians forming the House of Representatives and the Senate) in the referential sphere: 'We worked together, the White House and the Congress, to pass a significant supplemental.' This gives the impression that Bush is in complete control of the situation, that he has the unanimous backing of his administration and the US Congress, and that he is willing to retaliate militarily.

The plural third person pronoun in the nominative case is used nine times in the text, the plural third person pronoun in the accusative case is used six times, the plural third person pronoun in the genitive case (adjective) is used three times, and the plural third person pronoun in the genitive case (pronoun) is not used. The plural third person pronoun in the nominative case is used twice to refer to US citizens 'from all walks of life', but is subsequently used only in reference to non-US citizens. It is used five times to refer to the leaders of Pakistan, India and Saudi Arabia, and twice in reference to another social group: 'people have declared war on America, and they have made a terrible mistake'. At first, the identity of these 'people' seems clear: 'they' are those responsible for the attacks, along with 'those who encouraged them', those 'who house them', and 'those who comfort them', but the use of the word 'crusade' suggests otherwise.

The word 'crusade' was originally used to refer to any of several holy wars fought by Christians against Muslims in the Middle Ages. Although the word can now be used in a non-religious sense to refer to a series of actions carried out over a period of time for a particular cause, it still has strong religious connotations. The use of the word in this context makes the 'war on terrorism' sound like a religious war: one that once again pits Christians against Muslims. If we also take into account the repeated use of the word 'faith' throughout the text as well as references to prayer, mourning, 'God's good graces' and 'the Lord's Day', it now appears to be only Christian US citizens rather than US citizens 'from all walks of life' who are being included in the referential sphere and Muslims who are being identified as 'other'.

An article by Peter Ford in *The Christian Science Monitor* (19 September 2001) warned that Bush's allusion to a crusade against terrorism 'could spark a "clash of civilizations" between Christians and Muslims, sowing fresh winds of hatred and mistrust', and many spoke out in protest:

> His use of the word crusade was most unfortunate. It recalled the barbarous and unjust military operations against the Muslim world by Christian knights, who launched repeated attempts to capture Jerusalem over the course of several hundred years.
>
> (Grand Mufti Soheib Bensheikh, quoted in Ford, 2001)

> If this 'war' takes a form that affronts moderate Arab opinion, if it has the air of a clash of civilizations, there is a strong risk that it will contribute to Osama bin Laden's goal: a conflict between the Arab-Muslim world and the West.
>
> (*Le Monde* editorial, 18 September 2001)

> Bush is walking a fine line. The same black and white language he uses to rally Americans behind him is just the sort of language that risks splitting the international coalition he is trying to build. This confusion between politics and religion risks encouraging a clash of civilizations in a religious sense.
>
> (Dominique Moisi, political analyst with the French Institute for International Relations, quoted in Ford, 2001)

> It is their support for Washington's war that could be undermined by the sort of language on the president's lips. The whole tone is that of one civilization against another. It is a superior way of speaking and I fear the consequences – the world being divided into two between those who think themselves superior and the rest.
>
> (Hussein Amin, former Egyptian ambassador, quoted in Ford, 2001)

SUBHUMAN AND SUPERHUMAN

Like pronouns, adjectives can be used to construct favourable images of self and unfavourable images of the other. Before humans kill during wartime or support killing in their name, they must not only have a well-defined enemy, but an enemy that appears to be less than human, and adjectives play a significant role in the dehumanisation of the other. In Text 5: Today We Mourned, Tomorrow We Work (pp. 32–4), for example, Bush defines the other as evil and barbaric, and the self as good and civilised. The process of portraying one 'side' as good/superior and the other as bad/inferior is known as Manichaeanism, a clear example of which occurred during the Anglo-Boer War.

Between 1899 and 1902, Britain was involved in a bloody conflict with Dutch-descended Afrikaners (or Boers) in southern Africa. The Boer republics of the Transvaal and Orange Free State were established in the middle of the nineteenth century, but the discovery of gold in the Transvaal in 1884 lured countless numbers of British miners and prospectors to settle in the area. The Boers, who were principally farmers, resented this invasion of their land, and ill-feeling soon escalated into all-out war. In order to foster the belief in Britain and abroad that the Afrikaners were subhumans in need of civilising, they were commonly referred to in the British press as 'backward Boers' and 'dirty Dutchmen'.

In H. W. Wilson's *With the Flag to Pretoria* (1901), the Boers are described as a 'shabby, dirty, dilapidated lot of men with not a touch of soldierly smartness about them':

> As they came forth from their lairs, clad in ill-fitting garments of extra-ordinary incongruity, laden with parcels, bundles, teapots, and bottles; many with umbrellas and many with goloshes, those last refuges of the effeminate; in appearance a mob of frowsy vagrants; officers and men wondered that such a force had been able to hold back a splendidly disciplined British division for a whole day at Modder River, to repel at Magersfontein the desperate valour of the Highlanders.

All of the adjectives used to describe the Boers have extremely negative connotations. Not only are the Boer troops portrayed here as scruffy, filthy, unsoldierly, badly dressed, ladylike, ill-disciplined and cowardly, but the use of the word 'lairs' to describe where the men have been sheltering suggests that they are like rats and further strengthens the notion that the Boers are uncivilised and less than human. Although only the 'desperate valour of the Highlanders' and the splendid discipline of a single British division are mentioned, the reader is left with the impression that the British troops must be the exact antithesis of the Boers: smart, clean, soldierly, well-dressed, manly, disciplined and brave. The unfavourable description of the Boers also appears to suggest that the British are waging a just war against a subhuman foe. What is not mentioned here, however, is the fact that the Boers had just survived days upon days of some of the most intense artillery bombardments of the war huddled in hastily dug bomb-shelters. According to eyewitness accounts, furthermore, the British troops looked little better since they had been fighting for weeks in even worse conditions.

Perhaps the most straightforward way of dehumanising the other is to outwardly label 'them' as subhumans. This was the method preferred by Heinrich Himmler, Nazi Reichsführer-SS, head of the Gestapo and Waffen-SS, and Minister of the Interior during the Second World War. In *Der Untermensch* (1942), a German-produced racial propaganda pamphlet partially written by Himmler, all those who do not conform to the Nazi ideal of the Aryan master race (i.e. Slavs and Jews) are classified as 'Untermensch' (subhumans): 'Whether under the Tatars, or Peter, or Stalin, this people is born for the yoke.' Subhumans, it is explained, resemble humans in some respects, but are more closely related to lower orders of the animal kingdom. In Nazi ideology, the antonym of Untermensch is Übermensch (superhumans) – a term borrowed from German philosopher Friedrich Nietzsche's *Also Sprach Zarathustra* (1883) – and since, according to Nazi doctrine, Germans are superhuman, they should have no qualms about exterminating subhuman Jews or invading Russia in order to exploit its inferior Slavic population.

Activity

1   Find a variety of British and US newspaper and/or internet articles written before and shortly after the capture of Iraqi President Saddam Hussein by American forces on 13 December 2003.

2   Discuss the ways in which language is used to create a sense of otherness.

3   Which nouns and adjectives are most commonly used to describe Saddam Hussein in the British and American press?

4   What terms are used to describe the place where Saddam Hussein was
      captured and how do these affect the way in which Saddam Hussein
      himself is portrayed?

(See the commentary on p. 93.)

Extension

The 'Cold War' is the name given to the period of deep distrust, suspicion
and rivalry between nations with different political and ideological systems
that continued from the end of the Second World War until the dissolution
of the Soviet Union in the early 1990s. On one side were the Union of Soviet
Socialist Republics (USSR) and its allies, usually referred to as the Eastern bloc,
and on the other were the US and its allies, usually referred to as the Western
bloc. The US suspected the USSR of attempting to spread communism
throughout the world, whereas the USSR suspected the US of attempting to
stop revolutionary activity in other countries. Friction between the two sides
increased the likelihood of World War Three on a number of occasions.

1   Watch at least one of the following films produced during the Cold
      War: *High Treason* (1951); *The Manchurian Candidate* (1962); *Telefon*
      (1978); *Red Dawn* (1984).

2   Comment on the ways in which communists and/or communist
      sympathisers are represented as other in relation to non-communists.

3   In what ways are an 'us' (Western bloc) and 'them' (Eastern bloc) char-
      acterised?

FURTHER READING

Chilton, P. (1982) 'Nukespeak: Nuclear language, culture and propaganda' in
      C. Aubrey *Nukespeak: The media and the bomb*. London: Comedia.

Silberstein, S. (2002) *War of Words: Language, politics and 9/11*. London:
      Routledge.

Your country
needs you

This unit will analyse the interaction between verbal and visual English in military propaganda and will look, in particular, at the ways in which propagandists attempt to conceal the interested nature of verbal and visual representation during wartime. We do not all fall prey to propaganda, but those who do often feel that they have made a voluntary choice, even though they were never given a real chance to do so, and this unit will explore how propaganda works at both conscious and subconscious levels. It will begin with an analysis of propaganda posters and leaflets and will then focus on the use of verbal and visual English in military recruitment drives.

The word 'propaganda' comes from the Modern Latin 'congregatio de propaganda fide', meaning 'congregation for propagating the faith', and was first used in reference to a committee of cardinals responsible for foreign missions, founded by Pope Gregory XV in 1622. The *Oxford English Dictionary* (1989) defines 'propaganda' in its current general sense, dating from around the early twentieth century, as 'The systematic propagation of information or ideas by an interested party, especially in a tendentious way in order to encourage or instil a particular attitude or response.' Although propaganda, whether verbal or visual, is always highly manipulative in that its ultimate aim is to alter beliefs and/or behaviour, it was not uncommon to find the word used as a **synonym** of publicity in early twentieth century Europe:

> The term propaganda has not the sinister meaning in Europe which it has acquired in America. In European business offices the word means advertising or boosting generally.
>
> (George Seldes, *You Can't Print That! The truth behind the news*, 1929)

In short, propaganda was not regarded as biased, misleading or false information, as it often is today, but as harmless exaggeration. It was not until the Second World War that the word began to acquire **pejorative** connotations, and it is now a rarity to see or hear those working in politics, advertising, public relations, business or the military referring to their own written and/or spoken output as propaganda. As the American journalist Walter Lippmann famously remarked, however, propaganda always appears to be produced by 'them' and never 'us':

> We must remember that in time of war what is said on the enemy's side of the front is always propaganda, and what is said on our side of the front is truth and righteousness, the cause of humanity and a crusade for peace.
>
> (Quoted in J. Luskin's *Lippmann, Liberty and the Press*, 1972)

Propaganda is usually thought of in terms of spoken and written communication but can readily be found in a wide variety of forms. For example, a republican would see the Queen's head on British coins and banknotes as propaganda. (A royalist, of course, would have an entirely different view.) An anti-capitalist would see the McDonald's 'Golden Arches' logo as propaganda. (Again, the Managing Director of McDonald's would have a different view.) It is for this reason that we must now focus on English in both the verbal and visual channels of communication.

Activity

1 Are there any streets where you live named after famous battles that your country was involved in?

2 Would you classify these as propaganda?

Commentary

I live in Birmingham, the second largest city in England, and there are streets here named Trafalgar Road, Waterloo Road, Balaclava Road and Jutland Road. These are named after famous battles involving British armed forces. The Battle of Trafalgar (1805) was fought between the Royal Navy and the combined fleets of France and Spain; the Battle of Waterloo (1815) was one of the most decisive battles of the Napoleonic Wars; the Battle of Balaclava (1854) was the second major engagement of the Crimean War; and the Battle of Jutland (1916) was the greatest naval battle of the First World War. I would classify these as propaganda because they are 'interested': they each celebrate Britain's imperial past.

Propaganda is also usually associated with totalitarian regimes, such as Adolf Hitler's Germany or Joseph Stalin's Soviet Union, and it is perhaps a tribute to the success of propaganda produced by democratic governments that we naturally tend to associate it with the other rather than ourselves. It may, of course, be possible for governments to elicit the desired response through punitive measures. For Jews, Gypsies, homosexuals, Jehovah's Witnesses, Catholic priests and others, the threat of internment in a concentration camp in Hitler's Nazi Germany was ever-present, as was the threat of exile to Siberia in Stalin's Soviet Union, but neither of these would be considered propaganda. Although such threats may have helped these regimes to achieve their desired ends, the central element in propagandist inducements, as opposed to compulsion on the one side and blackmail on the other, is that they depend on verbal or visual communication (and agreement from the receiver) rather than concrete penalties.

To affect a person's behaviour by threatening them with violence is not propaganda, but if verbal or visual language is used to persuade a person to alter their behaviour, then the word becomes more appropriate. Propaganda can thus best be described as interested and deliberate. It aims to control or alter attitudes, not through physical violence, but through verbal or visual persuasion. If a propaganda campaign is to be successful, moreover, it must fulfil each of the following criteria outlined by D. Cartwright in 'Some Principles of Mass Persuasion' (1963):

- the message must be received by those who are to be influenced by it;

- the message must be accepted by the receiver as a constituent part of his/her **cognitive structure**;

43

◎   if the message does not correspond to the pre-existing cognitive structure, it will either be rejected or changed in such a way that it does correspond, or there will be a change in the cognitive structure;

◎   the behaviour which the propagandist wishes to encourage in the receiver must be recognized by him/her as a means of achieving an aim which is in his/her own interests;

◎   to bring about a specific behaviour the receiver's behavioural patterns must be controlled by an adequate motivational system, which, at the decisive moment, leads the receiver to the intended behaviour.

Each of the nations involved in the First World War used posters as a quick and effective way of ensuring that propagandistic messages and images were received by the majority of those who were intended to be influenced by them. Propaganda posters were used not only as a means of justifying each nation's involvement in the war, but also, as we shall see later in this unit, as a means of procuring the men, money and resources needed to sustain the military campaign. As stated on the firstworldwar.com website (www.firstworldwar.com/posters/):

> In countries such as Britain the use of propaganda posters was readily understandable: in 1914 she only possessed a professional army and did not have in place a policy of national service, as was standard in other major nations such as France and Germany. Posters commonly urged wartime thrift, and were vocal in seeking funds from the general public via subscription to various war bond schemes (usually with great success).

However, many First World War posters were a more insidious form of propaganda.

Activity

Text 6: The Hun and the Home is a British propaganda poster produced during the First World War.

1   What sort of information was the poster intended to disseminate?

2   What sort of attitude or response were the propagandists hoping to encourage?

3   How closely does this piece of propaganda follow D. Cartwright's criteria?

Text 6: The Hun and the Home

Commentary

The poster attempts to manipulate the emotions of the receiver (i.e. the average English person) by warning what will happen to England if 'THE MEN WHO HAVE SAVED YOU' (i.e. British and Commonwealth soldiers) are not fully supported by those at home. It does so by presenting an idealistic image of 'A BIT OF [rural] ENGLAND' and juxtaposing this with a war-ravaged 'BIT OF BELGIUM'. As Sharon Goodman and David Graddol point out in their book *Redesigning English: New texts, new identities* (1996), given/new structures such as this are commonly found in both verbal and visual English:

> In verbal English . . . the given is what comes first in the clause and the new what comes last, and what, usually, has the greatest stress. In other words, given and new are realized sequentially (through 'before' and 'after'). These can be transcoded in images by use of the horizontal axis. In images, given and new are represented spatially, through 'left' and 'right'. A vast number of advertisements in English use the visual axis in this way, positioning the taken-for-granted, 'already understood' information on the left and the new information on the right. The left side of the advertisement often outlines the problem, or given situation, while the right side shows the product.

The following military metaphor, taken from the *Daily Star* newspaper (22 January 1992), is used by Goodman and Graddol as an example of a verbal given/new structure: 'It's time to stop the phoney war and start the real battle.' The visual given/new structure in the poster suggests that England (the given, taken-for-granted, 'already understood' information on the left) will end up like Belgium (the new information on the right) if the English people are not supportive enough. The 'BIT OF ENGLAND', to put it another way, is 'before': what 'THE MEN' have been fighting for, and the 'BIT OF BELGIUM' is 'after': the possible product of public complacency.

The main propagandistic message of the poster is that all English people should contribute to the war effort and the visual given/new structure encourages the receiver to believe that this behaviour is in his/her own best interests. This visual given/new structure is reinforced by the verbal given/new structure of plural first and third person pronouns in the genitive case: OUR Homes are secure/THEIR Homes are destroyed; OUR Mothers & Wives safe/THEIR Women are murdered & worse; OUR Children still play and fear no harm/THEIR Children are dead or slaves, and it is clearly only English people who are being included in the referential sphere. Although the threat of invasion and destruction is not propaganda, it acts as a powerful motivational system controlling the receiver's behavioural patterns.

46

There is no visual representation of the other in Text 6: The Hun and the Home, but the language of the poster conjures up a strong mental image. 'Hun', a 'loaded' derogatory word for a person of German descent, is used in order to dehumanise the other and encourage the receiver to accept the propagandistic message as a constituent part of his/her cognitive structure. The **denotation** of the word 'Hun' in *Webster's Dictionary of Phrase and Fable* (1977) is: 'An uncivilized brute; from the barbarian tribe of Huns who invaded the East Roman Empire in the 4th and 5th centuries.' It still carries strong negative cultural connotations and those reading the poster during the First World War would have automatically associated its use with barbarism and brutality. The propagandistic message thus reinforces pre-existing German stereotypes. The comparative adjective 'worse', furthermore, is used to imply that German soldiers are not only warmongers, slave-traders and murderers of innocent men, women and children, but also rapists.

Activity

Text 7: Red Cross or Iron Cross is another First World War British propaganda poster.

1   Comment on the interplay between verbal and visual communication in the poster.

2   How does the poster attempt to manipulate the emotions of the receiver?

3   What is the main propagandistic message?

4   How do those responsible for producing the poster encourage the receiver to accept the propagandistic message as a constituent part of his/her cognitive structure?

5   What sort of behaviour do the propagandists wish to elicit in the receiver?

6   How is the receiver encouraged to believe that this behaviour is in his/her own best interests?

7   What is the motivational system in this instance?

8   Comment on the use of language used to describe 'the other' in the poster.

9   How are Germans represented visually?

10 In *Eats, Shoots and Leaves* (2003), Lynne Truss states that 'inverted commas are sometimes known as scare quotes'. Comment on the use of inverted commas in the poster.

11 The language in the poster is obviously 'interested' (see Unit two: Verbal armoury), but how do the propagandists attempt to conceal this?

47

Text 7: Red Cross or Iron Cross

(There is no commentary for this activity.)

On 2 August 1990, Iraqi forces under the leadership of Saddam Hussein invaded and seized control of neighbouring Kuwait. President George H. W. Bush ordered US forces to the Persian Gulf in order to defend Saudi Arabia against attack. Eventually, 30 nations joined the military coalition arrayed against Iraq, with a further 18 countries supplying economic and humanitarian assistance. This operation was known as Desert Shield. On 17 January 1991, when it became clear that Saddam Hussein would not withdraw from Kuwait, Desert Shield became Desert Storm.

Activity

Text 8: Airdrop Propaganda Leaflet is one of many airdrop propaganda leaflets produced by the US Army Department of Psychological Warfare during Operation Desert Shield/Desert Storm. Tens of thousands of these leaflets were dropped between 1990 and 1991.

1   Where do you think this leaflet was airdropped and who was the target readership?

2   What propagandistic messages are there in the leaflet?

3   What is the main message of the leaflet?

4   Does the message attempt to manipulate with emotion, reason or both?

5   Describe how this type of manipulation may have worked.

6   Arabic has words meaning 'OOPS' and 'THUD'. Why did the US Army Department of Psychological Warfare choose to use English words?

7   What type of response was the US military hoping to elicit?

Text 8: Airdrop Propaganda Leaflet

(See the commentary on pp. 93–4.)

RECRUITMENT

Once we consider the fact that former designers and advertisers were among the most successful wartime propagandists, it is hardly surprising to find advertising techniques such as verbal and visual given/new structures being used in wartime propaganda posters. As Dave Saunders points out in his book *Twentieth Century Advertising* (1999):

> By the end of World War One, governments of the leading powers had realized the potential role of advertising in the dissemination of information and the rallying of support. Posters were the primary medium of mass communication and many artists and designers were called on to reverse their usual role of promoting products and use their persuasive talents to encourage the public to spend less and to conserve resources. The creative process required was much the same, but the sense of urgency that war brings created a crop of innovative ideas and high-quality artwork that was frequently copied and had a major effect on later advertising.

Alfred Leete was one such former designer who turned his hand to wartime propaganda. Leete's famous Lord Kitchener poster design (see Text 9: Britons) first appeared on the front cover of the weekly magazine *London Opinion* in September 1914, a month after Britain had declared war on Germany. The Parliamentary Recruiting Committee altered the wording slightly and it went on to become perhaps the most well-known wartime propaganda poster of all time – its basic design being used to sell a wide variety of different goods and services worldwide.

Text 9: Britons

To the majority of British people in 1914, Kitchener's face and trademark handlebar moustache would have been instantly recognisable, hence the omission of Kitchener's name in the poster. The face, in other words, spoke for itself. Lord Kitchener of Khartoum (1850–1916), Secretary of State for War in 1914, had a distinguished military career and his cele- brated exploits in Sudan, South Africa and India made him a prominent public figure. He was renowned as a tough and uncompromising military commander who could always be relied upon to get the job done, and it is precisely because of these no-nonsense connotations that his image was chosen by Leete as a symbol of the national will to win.

The most striking and effective aspect of the poster, however, is the way in which it employs **direct address** in both verbal and visual modes. Direct address, as opposed to indirect address, is used to attract attention. In the following examples of verbal direct address, nouns or pronouns are used to attract the receiver's attention:

Waiter, there's a fly in my soup.

Hey, you, what the hell do you think you're playing at?

Leete's poster uses a plural noun, the plural second person pronoun in the accusative case and the plural second person pronoun in the geni- tive case (adjective) to address the receivers (i.e. BRITONS) directly:

BRITONS [Lord Kitchener] WANTS YOU

JOIN YOUR COUNTRY'S ARMY!

The poster also uses visual direct address to attract the attention of the receivers. Kitchener's image is not only looking straight at the receivers, but also pointing straight at the receivers with his finger. The way in which English in both the verbal and visual channels of communica- tion combine to convey the same meaning reinforces the propagandistic message in the strongest possible way.

Activity

Text 10: Join the Elite is a relatively recent British Army recruitment adver- tisement that appeared in the West Midlands *Jobs and Training Weekly* newspaper (11–17 July). As in Texts 6, 7, 8 and 9, Text 10: Join the Elite is multimodal (i.e. it uses both verbal and visual language).

1   Does the verbal language address the receiver directly?

2   Does the visual language address the receiver directly?

3   Comment on the use of verbs in the imperative mood.

Text 10: Join the Elite

JOIN THE ELITE

To be part of Britain's elite commandos on a part time basis, join the Royal Marines Commandos. Royel Marines Reserve Merseyside has detachments in Liverpool, Manchester & Birmingham.

For an information pack call 0800 783 9529

To apply you must be male and aged between 17 and 32

(There is no commentary for this activity.)

Alfred Leete's Kitchener poster was adapted for the US by James Montgomery Flagg (see Text 11: I Want You For U.S. Army) and has since been resurrected repeatedly in a variety of different guises (see Text 12: His Country Needs You).

1 Comment on the differences between Flagg's US adaptation and Leete's original version in terms of both verbal and visual language.

2 Discuss the possible reasons for the alterations that Flagg made.

3 Flagg himself donned a hat and fake beard to serve as the model for Uncle Sam. Why do you think he chose to do this rather than adapt earlier characterisations of Uncle Sam as a passive old man?

4 Text 12: His Country Needs You appeared on the front page of the *Daily Mirror*, a British tabloid newspaper, on Tuesday, 19 October 2004. Comment on the differences between this and Flagg's poster in terms of both verbal and visual language.

5 Why do you think the *Daily Mirror* chose to adapt Flagg's poster?

Text 11: I Want You For U.S. Army

Text 12: His Country Needs You

(There is no commentary for this activity.)

Extension

1   Research original US First and Second World War posters, either on the firstworldwar.com website or any others that you can find on the internet.

2   Micah Wright is a US author and artist who 'remixes' war propaganda. Visit his website at www.micahwright.com/index3.htm or obtain a copy of his book *You Back the Attack! We'll Bomb Who We Want!* (2003).

3   How and why does Micah Wright subvert the original propagandistic message of wartime posters?

FURTHER READING

Cantwell, J. (1989) *Images of War: British posters 1939–45*. London: HMSO.

Keen, Sam (1991) *Faces of the Enemy: Reflections of the hostile imagination*. San Francisco, CA: HarperSanFrancisco.

Kress, G. and Van Leeuwen, T. (1996) *Reading Images: The grammar of visual design*. London: Routledge.

Rickards, M. (1968) *Posters of the First World War*. London: Evelyn Adams Mackay.

Van Leeuwen, T. and Jewitt, C. (2001) *Handbook of Visual Analysis*. London: Sage.

Live from
the front

In the previous unit we looked at the ways in which both verbal and visual language have been used by the military to recruit and bolster support for military campaigns. In this unit we will compare and contrast media coverage of war with the language used in official war reports. Since, as Martin Montgomery points out in *An Introduction to Language and Society* (1995), 'One particularly crucial set of patterns [which has fundamental consequences for the mode of representation] is concerned with representing actions and their concomitant persons and circumstances', this unit will focus primarily on the ways in which actions and the people responsible for these actions are represented verbally. We will begin with an analysis of the grammatical choices made to represent actions and agency in war journalism and then move on to look at texts produced by the military in the second part of the unit.

The terms **active**, **middle** and **passive voice** will be used frequently in this unit. Voice is determined by whether the subject of a clause is the **agent** of the action or affected by the action of a **transitive verb**. In the active voice, the subject of a clause is the agent of the action of a transitive verb. In the following clause, for example, 'The dog' is the subject (S) and agent of the action, 'bit' is the action of a transitive verb (V) and 'the postman' is the direct **object** (O):

```
        S        V        O
The dog | bit | the postman.
```

In the passive voice, the subject of a clause is affected by the action of a transitive verb. In the following clause, for example, 'The postman' is the subject (S) affected by the action of a transitive verb, 'was bitten' is the action of a transitive verb (V) and 'by the dog' is the **adjunct** (A) and agent of the action:

```
        S            V            A
The postman | was bitten | by the dog.
```

Passive voice can be used in a number of different **tenses**:

Passive	Simple	Progressive
Present	is bitten	is being bitten
Past	was bitten	was being bitten
Future	will be bitten	
Present perfect	has been bitten	
Past perfect	had been bitten	
Future perfect	will have been bitten	

(Note: future, present perfect, past perfect and future perfect progressive are also possible in the passive voice but uncommon.)

Most grammar books list the following as reasons for using the passive voice:

◎   the agent is unknown (Last night all of my belongings <u>were stolen</u>);

◎   the agent is unimportant (The pyramids of Egypt <u>were built</u> as a burial place for the pharaoh god-kings);

◎   the agent is common knowledge (Tony Blair <u>was re-elected</u> with another landslide majority in the 2001 General Election).

There is, however, one further reason why the passive voice is used – one that is of direct relevance to the subject of this book. The passive voice can also be used if the speaker or writer wishes to control the focus of attention. Compare, for example, the following sentences:

1   I broke the window.

2   The window broke.

58

3   The window was broken.

4   The window was broken by me.

If the person responsible for breaking the window was asked what had happened, they could choose to answer using the first option (active voice) and admit responsibility for breaking the window, or they could attempt to evade responsibility by choosing one of the other three options. In the second option (middle voice) there is no mention of an external human agent who caused the window to break: the window appears to have broken itself. The third and fourth options are both in the passive voice, but the third option (known as a short or **agentless passive**) enables the speaker to leave out the agent altogether. In other words, when using the passive voice the speaker or writer can choose whether to make the agent of the action explicit or not.

Activity

1   Find articles covering the same event in two or three different newspapers, preferably printed on the same day.

2   Compare and contrast the way(s) in which the newspapers portray the event.

3   Are there any major differences in the **angle of representation**? If so, how would you account for these differences?

(There is no commentary for this activity.)

You more than likely found that not all sections of the media want to represent events in exactly the same way. This is because different newspapers, magazines, websites, television channels and radio stations have their own agendas that affect the way events are reported. Any report of any event – whether it is produced by the mass media or, as we shall see, the armed forces or other official sources – is selective because of the interested nature of linguistic representation (see Unit one: Fighting talk). Some sections of the media are obviously biased and make no attempt to hide this fact from their readership or audience, but even the BBC, which (according to the BBC Editorial Policy written by Mark

Damazer, the Deputy Director of BBC News) 'sees its audience as citizens who have the right to independent and impartial information' (news.bbc.co.uk/aboutbbcnews/hi/editorial_policy), is incapable of representing events objectively.

Activity

1   Find articles covering the same conflict in a number of different newspapers.

2   Make a list of the verbs used in the passive voice in the articles.

3   Do these verbs have anything in common? If so, how would you account for these similarities?

(There is no commentary for this activity.)

In *The Longman Grammar of Spoken and Written English* (1999), Biber *et al.* list the following verbs as occurring over 40 times per million words of news in the passive voice: *be* + accused; announced; arrested; beaten; believed; charged; delighted; hit; injured; jailed; killed; named; released; revealed; shot; sold. You may have noticed that many of the verbs you listed have negative connotations too. This is because the field of hard news, as opposed to the field of soft news, relates mainly to wars, disasters, murders, etc. Alan Bell distinguishes between hard and soft news in *The Language of News Media* (1991) thus:

> Newsworkers' basic distinction is between hard news and features. Hard news is their staple product: reports of accidents, conflicts, crimes, announcements, discoveries and other events which have occurred or come to light since the previous issue of their paper or programme. The one-off, unscheduled events such as fires and disasters are sometimes called 'spot news'. The opposite to hard news is 'soft' news, which is not time-bound to immediacy. Features are the most obvious case of soft news. These are longer 'articles' rather than 'stories' covering immediate events. They provide background, sometimes 'editorialize' (carry the writer's personal opinions), and are usually bylined with the writer's name. ... For both newsworkers and researchers, the boundaries between hard and soft

news are unclear . . . journalists spend much of their energy trying to find an angle which will present what is essentially soft news in hard news terms. Journalists and media researchers both recognize hard news as the core news product, the typical against which other copy will be measured. Hard news is also the place where a distinctive news style will be found if anywhere.

Consider now the following excerpts from 'hard news' articles printed in the *Daily Mail*:

US bomb kills 30 at Afghan wedding

17:48pm, 1st July 2002   At least 30 members of an Afghan wedding party were killed and many more wounded when a US plane bombed a village in the central province of Uruzgan today, Afghan officials and residents said. The bombing happened today in a village in the rugged, mountainous region 175km (105 miles) northeast of the southern city of Kandahar, residents said.

US planes launch Afghan bombing raid

09:58am, 17th February 2002   US aircraft launched a bombing raid in eastern Afghanistan, apparently in support of Afghan government forces trying to break up a clash between tribal factions, a Pakistan-based news agency said on Sunday. The private Afghan Islamic Press (AIP) said a US plane bombed the Farm Bagh area, some 30 km (19 miles) east of Khost town, on Saturday evening after security forces loyal to the interim government tried to stop a tribal battle.

Six dead in Beirut car bomb blast

11:50am, 14th February 2005   A suspected car bomb blast rocked Beirut's waterfront, setting several cars on fire and killing at least six people. TV showed a man on fire falling out of a burning car window. Witnesses and a politician said the blast apparently targeted former Prime Minster Rafik Hariri's motorcade.

All three attempt to shift the reader's attention away from the agents of the actions, but do so in different ways. In the first text, the past simple tense in the passive voice (were killed/wounded) is used to de-emphasise the role of the agents (US soldiers) in the action (the killing and wounding of members of an Afghan wedding party). If rewritten in the active voice, the first clause ('At least 30 members of an Afghan wedding party were killed and many more wounded') would read: 'US soldiers killed at least 30 members of an Afghan wedding party and wounded many more', but, since the editorial board of the *Daily Mail* was firmly in favour of the US-led invasion of Afghanistan in 2001, it is hardly surprising that an agentless passive construction was chosen in this instance. When responding to news of the deaths, White House spokesman Ari Fleischer also chose to use the past simple tense in the passive voice: 'The president is concerned about reports from Afghanistan that innocent lives were lost in the conduct of joint US–Afghan military operations in Uruzgan province.' Again, the focus of attention is shifted away from the agents through strategic grammatical choice.

Middle voice is used in the second clause of the first text: 'a US plane bombed a village in the central province of Uruzgan today'. Unlike the first clause, where human agency (although not specified) is implied, the second clause foregrounds technology (a US plane) and backgrounds human agency altogether. This strategy is also used in the title of the article: 'US bomb kills 30 at Afghan wedding.' When questioned about the deaths, US Defence Secretary Donald Rumsfeld also chose to avoid naming a human agent: 'There cannot be the use of that kind of firepower and not have mistakes and errant weapons exist. It's going to happen. It always has and it always will.' Not only does Rumsfeld refuse to accept responsibility for the existence of 'errant' US weaponry, but he also tries to make the deaths sound like a natural and acceptable outcome of war. His 'It's going to happen' comment is similar in many respects to the beginning of the second sentence of the first text: 'The bombing happened', as well as a subsequent comment Rumsfeld made at a press conference on 11 April 2003 when questioned about the looting of Baghdad: 'Stuff happens.' All three are examples of middle voice that prevent any sense of external agency. It is as if the killing, wounding, bombing and looting all happened naturally without any impulsion from external agents, and as if there is nothing anybody can do to stop them happening again.

Activity

1   Analyse the two other *Daily Mail* texts above in a similar way, labelling the verbs/verbal groups and discussing the lexico-grammatical choices made.

2   Is agency attributed?

3   If so, who or what is made the agent?

4   Rewrite both texts in the active voice, adding a human agent where necessary.

5   Comment on the differences between these and the original versions.

Commentary

Middle voice is used throughout the second text. According to the title, the bombing raid was launched by 'US planes' rather than the US military or government. (Interestingly, it is 'Afghan government forces' who are being supported but not US government forces who are supporting them.) 'US aircraft' are held responsible in the first clause of the text, but a single 'US plane' is said to have 'bombed the Farm Bagh area' in the second sentence. Agency is thus attributed to technology. If rewritten with a human agent added, the text might read something like this:

> **US government forces launch Afghan bombing raid**
> 09:58am, 17th February 2002   US government forces launched a bombing raid in eastern Afghanistan, apparently in support of Afghan government forces trying to break up a clash between tribal factions, a Pakistan-based news agency said on Sunday. The private Afghan Islamic Press (AIP) said US government forces bombed the Farm Bagh area, some 30 km (19 miles) east of Khost town, on Saturday evening after security forces loyal to the interim government tried to stop a tribal battle.

When compared to the original text, the rewritten text makes US government involvement sound far less benevolent. It now sounds as if this was indeed an ideologically driven act.

The third text utilises a grammatical possibility that we have not yet considered: **nominalisation**. Nominalisation is the process of turning what is typically a verb into a noun. When a verb is nominalised, it becomes an abstract concept rather than a concrete action with direct consequences (in this case, the consequences are the 'rocking' of Beirut's waterfront, the setting on fire of several cars, the deaths of at least six people, the setting on fire of a man and the targeting of former Prime Minister Rafik Hariri's motorcade). It is not human beings, but a blast that rocks the waterfront, sets cars on fire and kills people. It is not television executives, but a TV that chooses to show 'a man on fire falling out of a burning car window'. It is not people, but a blast that targets the former Prime Minister's motorcade. This creates agents that are abstract grammatical entitities and once again sidelines human agency. According to Annabelle Lukin in *Reporting*

War: Grammar as covert operation (www.fair.org.au/modules.php?name=
News&file=article&sid=31, link no longer available):

> This kind of grammar is part of the syndrome of features through which
> expressions like 'collateral damage' [see Unit two: Verbal armoury]
> become possible. It is also fundamental to the tenor of statements like
> 'Our direct attacks against regime command-control, communications
> and integrated air defence continue and included attacks against
> several targets of opportunity yesterday,' from Brigadier General
> Vincent Brooks, who provided the daily briefings to journalists gathered
> at US Central Command [during the war on Iraq].

Activity

The following texts are excerpts from articles printed in the US newspaper,
the *Washington Post*. The first, written by John Ward Anderson, was printed
on 21 October 2003. The second, written by Molly Moore, was printed on
20 October 2003.

1   Compare and contrast the titles of the articles.

2   Rewrite the titles of the articles in as many different ways as possible.

3   Comment on the possible reasons why these other options were not
    chosen by the journalists.

4   What does the angle of representation in the titles of these articles
    suggest about the newspaper's attitude towards Arab–Israeli relations?

5   Analyse the remainder of the texts.

6   Does your analysis alter or support your answer to question number
    four?

7   Comment on the use of the words 'gunmen' and 'soldiers' in the
    second text.

Strikes by Israeli Aircraft Kill at Least 11 in Gaza
At least 11 Palestinians were killed and more than 135 were injured
on Monday in five attacks by Israeli military aircraft on Palestinian
militant targets in the Gaza Strip, Palestinian hospital officials and
witnesses said.

Palestinian Gunmen Attack West Bank Patrol
Palestinian gunmen ambushed a group of Israeli soldiers on a foot
patrol near a Palestinian village in the West bank on Sunday night,
killing three and injuring a fourth, according to Israeli military officials.

Commentary

In the first title, the action of striking has been nominalised in order to create abstract rather than human agency. It is the strikes that did the killing, not the Israeli aircraft, military or government. The title can be rewritten in a number of different ways using the active ('Israeli Soldiers Kill at Least 11 in Gaza'), middle ('Israeli Airstrikes Kill at Least 11 in Gaza') or passive voice ('At Least 11 Killed in Gaza by Israeli Airstrikes'), but the chosen title makes neither human agency nor the nationality of the victims explicit. In contrast, the title of the second text leaves readers in no doubt about the nationality of the human agents or 'gunmen', even though the middle voice ('Palestinian Ambush Kills Israeli Soldiers'), long passive ('West Bank Patrol Attacked by Palestinian Gunmen') and agentless passive ('West Bank Patrol Attacked') are possible alternatives.

The past simple passive tense (were killed/were injured) is used twice in the first text. This emphasises those ('At least 11 Palestinians') affected by the action of the transitive verbs 'kill' and 'injure', de-emphasises the role of the agent (the Israeli military) in the action, and reinforces the sense already established in the title that 'Israeli military aircraft' rather than Israeli military personnel were responsible. The past simple active tense (ambushed) is used in the first clause of the second text, followed by 'killing' and 'injuring'. These two present participles are both active. Once again, readers are left in no doubt about who is doing the ambushing, killing and injuring. The fact that the newspaper is unwilling to attribute agency to Israelis in the first text but willing to attribute agency to Palestinians in the second gives the overall impression of pro-Israeli bias.

Other sources appear to offer a completely different angle of representation. In July 2003, HonestReporting, a media watch group established to monitor anti-Israeli bias, released a study of headlines produced by Reuters, an international multi-media news agency. According to the Honest-Reporting study (www.honestreporting.com), in articles covering the Arab–Israeli conflict where Israelis were responsible for committing violent acts, the active voice was used to attribute agency to Israelis in 100 per cent of the headlines. For example, 'Israeli Troops Shoot Dead Palestinian in W. Bank.' In articles covering the Arab–Israeli conflict where Palestinians were responsible for committing violent acts, on the other hand, the active voice was used to attribute agency to Palestinians in only 33 per cent of the headlines. Reuters also appears to favour the portrayal of Palestinian diplomats as pursuing peace but ultimately frustrated by their obstinate Israeli counterparts: 'Palestinians Urge Israel to Free Prisoners'; 'Israel Sets Tough Terms for Prisoner Release.' The study concludes that Reuters (as opposed to the angle of representation in the *Washington Post* texts above) invariably portrays Israelis as aggressors and Palestinians as hapless victims.

OFFICIAL REPORTS

It should by now be clear that, when reading, watching or listening to war coverage, it is important to be able to distinguish between a judgement, which includes judgemental language and expresses an unverifiable opinion, and a report, which does not include judgemental language and is a verifiable statement. The following sentence, for example, uses the **superlative** form of the adjective 'explosive': 'A serious new flare-up of military conflict has taken place in the Near East, which, as a result of the Israeli aggression of 1967, became one of the most explosive parts of the world.' This expresses an opinion that it would not be possible to verify and is therefore a judgement rather than a report. In the following sentence, on the other hand, United Nations observers are cited as sources: 'United Nations observers reported seeing Egyptians crossing into the Sinai Desert at five points along the 103-mile canal front; Syrian troops were spotted moving into Israel over the central section of the Golan Heights cease-fire line by other U.N. teams.' Since this excludes judgemental language and includes a source that could be checked, it appears to be a report rather than an opinion.

It should be remembered, however, that some statements may not be classifiable simply as reports or judgements. Official reports themselves, moreover, may or may not be true. For example, '"We will find Osama bin Laden and bring him to justice," said a Pentagon official,' may be classified as a report, since verifying that a Pentagon official made this statement is probably possible, but the statement itself is a prediction and can therefore be classified as a judgement. Again, it is probably possible to verify that the following statement was made by a professor of Soviet Studies: '"Nuclear deterrence prevented Soviet aggression," said a professor of Soviet studies.' Citing the professor as an authoritative source appears to make the statement a report, but what is said rests entirely on unverifiable inferences drawn by the professor, so this statement can also be classified as a judgement.

Activity

The American War of Independence (1775–83) was fought between Britain and revolutionaries from thirteen of its North American colonies. It eventually resulted in the overthrow of British rule and the establishment of the United States of America. Text 13: *Salem Gazette* and Text 14: *London Gazette* are excerpts from newspaper accounts of the first battle of the American War of Independence on 19 April 1775 at Lexington. The first text was printed in the North American *Salem Gazette* on 25 April 1775. The second was printed in the British *London Gazette* on 10 June 1775.

1   Read both accounts and identify three judgements and three reports from each text. (You may find it useful to draw up a table with two columns, one headed 'judgements', the other headed 'reports'.)

2   Do the texts differ in angle of representation?

3   If so, in what ways do the accounts differ?

4   How would you explain these differences?

Text 13: *Salem Gazette*

AT LEXINGTON, six miles below Concord, a company of militia, of about one hundred men, mustered near the meeting-house; the [British] troops came in sight of them just before sunrise; and running within a few rods of them, the Commanding Officer accosted the Militia in words to this effect: 'Disperse, you rebels – throw down your arms and disperse'; upon which the Troops huzzaed [*sic*], and immediately one or two officers discharged their pistols, which were instantaneously followed by the firing of four or five of the soldiers and then there seemed to be a general discharge from the whole body; eight of our men were killed and nine wounded. ... In Lexington, the enemy set fire to Deacon Joseph Loring's house and barn, Mrs. Mullikin's house and shop, and Mr. Joshua Bond's house and shop which were all consumed. ... They pillaged almost every house and passed by, breaking and destroying doors, windows, glasses, etc., and carrying off clothing and other valuable effects. ... But the savage barbarity exercised upon the bodies of our unfortunate brethren who fell, is almost incredible; not content with shooting down the unarmed, aged and infirm, they disregarded the cries of the wounded, killing them without mercy, and mangling their bodies in the most shocking manner. ... We have the pleasure to say, that, notwithstanding the highest provocations given by the enemy, not one instance of cruelty, that we have heard of, was committed by our victorious militia.

Text 14: *London Gazette*

LIEUTENANT-COLONEL SMITH finding, after he had advanced some miles on his march, that the country had been alarmed by the firing of guns and ringing of bells, dispatched six companies of light infantry, in order to secure two bridges on different roads beyond Concord, who upon their arrival at Lexington, found a body of the country people under arms, on a green close to the road; and upon the King's Troops marching up to them, in order to inquire the reason for their being so assembled, they went off in great confusion, and several guns were fired upon the King's Troops from behind a stone wall, and also from the meeting-house and other houses, by which one man was wounded, and Major Pitcairn's horse shot in two places. In consequence of this attack by the rebels, the troops returned the fire and killed several of them . . . such was the cruelty and barbarity of the rebels that they scalped and cut off the ears of some of the wounded men who fell into their hands.

(See the commentary on pp. 94–5.)

Newsworkers as well as those responsible for producing official war reports often cite sources in order to strengthen the authority of what they are saying. In the three *Daily Mail* and two *Washington Post* texts (pp. 61 and 64), for example, residents, news agencies, witnesses, politicians, hospital officials and military officials are cited as sources, but this is not always the case. The following text appeared in the online edition of *The New York Post* on 24 February 2003:

HUNT-AND-KILL SQUADS SET TO TAKE OUT
SADDAM & SONS
WASHINGTON – Special hunter-killer teams and aircraft would target strongman Saddam Hussein – and his two evil sons – within 8 hours of the launch of any military campaign, *The Post* has learned.

The moves would include a series of massive, surgical airstrikes and commando raids in the opening hours of the action. Specially trained operatives would target Saddam, sons Uday and Qusay and other key aides.

Qusay, who heads Saddam's personal Republican Guard unit, has orders to unleash weapons of mass destruction should something happen to his father, according to British intelligence.

Saddam's eldest son, Uday, is said to command Iraq's vicious paramilitary groups in charge of sabotaging infrastructure, such as bridges, and committing atrocities against their country's own civilians to blame on the United States.

In the past, Uday has been accused of personally brutally beating Iraqi Olympic athletes, as well as having ties to terrorists. He also is considered the money man who helps fund Saddam's regime.

Apart from a single reference to British intelligence in the third paragraph, the writer fails to cite a source for many of the assertions made in the article and frequently resorts to the passive voice as a method of avoiding doing so. Saddam Hussein's eldest son, for example, 'is said to command Iraq's vicious paramilitary groups', but no indication is given of who said this. We are also told that Hussein's other son 'has been accused of personally brutally beating Iraqi Olympic athletes' and 'is considered the money man who helps fund Saddam's regime', but agency is not attributed in either instance. Even the British intelligence reference raises questions. Has British intelligence ever made such a public statement? If not, then where did the *New York Post* actually get its information from? The question of what happened to those 'weapons of mass destruction' is also begging to be asked.

Activity

On 22 April 1861, a clash between Union soldiers and secessionists (civilians who supported the withdrawal of southern states from the Union in 1860) in Baltimore resulted in what is commonly accepted to be the first bloodshed of the American Civil War (1861–5). The Sixth Massachusetts Militia, who were one of the first regiments to respond to President Abraham Lincoln's call for Unionist troops, arrived in Baltimore by train, en route to Washington. Because the railway did not pass through the city, horse-drawn carriages had to take the Massachusetts infantrymen from one end of Baltimore to the other. An angry crowd tried to stop the regiment reaching Washington, blocking the roads, smashing the windows of the carriages, and forcing the soldiers to get out and march through the streets. The following official report (Text 15: Conflict in Baltimore), written by Colonel Edward F. Jones of the Sixth Massachusetts Militia, details what happened next.

69

1   Comment on the prominent angle of representation in the text.

2   Identify the verbs/verbal groups in the text and label them as either active or passive.

3   Can you suggest any reasons why the passive voice is used in certain parts of the text but not in others?

4   Rewrite all of the passive verbs/verbal groups in the active voice, adding a suitable agent where necessary. How does this version compare with the original?

5   Which parts of the text would you classify as judgements and which would you classify as reports?

6   Comment on the use of the word 'mob' to describe the secessionists.

Text 15: Conflict in Baltimore

Conflict in Baltimore, Md.

Report of Col. Edward F. Jones, Sixth Massachusetts Militia.

HDQRS. 6TH REGIMENT, 3D BRIG., 2D DIV., M. V. M.,
Capitol, Washington, April 22, 1861.

Brigade Maj. WILLIAM H. CLEMENCE

In accordance with Special Orders, No. 6, I proceeded with my command towards the city of Washington, leaving Boston on the evening of the 17th April, arrived in New York on the morning of the 18th, and proceeded to Philadelphia, reaching that place on the same evening.

On our way John Brady, of Company H, Lowell, was taken insane, and deeming it unsafe to have him accompany the regiment, I left him at Delanco, N. J., with J. C. Buck, with directions that he should telegraph Mayor Sargent, of Lowell, as to the disposition of him, and we proceeded thence to Baltimore, reaching that place at noon on the 19th. After leaving Philadelphia I received intimation that our passage through the city of Baltimore would be resisted. I caused ammunition to be distributed and arms loaded, went personally through the cars, and issued the following order, viz: The regiment will march through Baltimore in column of sections, arms at will. You will undoubtedly be insulted, abused, and, perhaps, assaulted, to which you must pay no attention whatever, but march with your faces square to the front, and pay no attention to the mob, even if they throw stones, bricks, or other missiles; but if you are fired upon and any one of you is hit, your officers will order you to fire. Do not fire into any promiscuous crowds, but select any man whom you may see aiming at you, and be sure you drop him.

Reaching Baltimore, horses were attached the instant that the locomotive was detached, and the cars were driven at a rapid pace across the city. After the cars containing seven companies had reached the Washington depot the track behind them was barricaded, and the cars containing band and the following companies viz: Company C, of Lowell, Captain Follansbee; Company D, of Lowell, Captain Hart; Company I, of Lawrence, Captain Pickering, and Company L, of Stoneham, Captain Dike, were vacated, and they proceeded but a short distance before they were furiously attacked by a shower of missiles, which came faster as they advanced. They increased their steps to double-quick, which seemed to infuriate the mob, as it evidently impressed the mob with the idea that the soldiers dared not fire or had no ammunition, and pistol-shots were numerously fired into the ranks, and one soldier fell dead. The order 'Fire' was given, and it was executed. In consequence, several of the mob fell, and the soldiers again advanced hastily.

(There is no commentary for this activity.)

Activity

Text 16: The Campaign is an excerpt from an official report entitled *Operations in Iraq: First reflections* produced by the British Ministry of Defence (MoD). It was first published on the MoD website (www.mod.uk/publications/iraq_lessons) in July 2003 and summarises the extent of British military involvement in Iraq.

1   Skim-read the text. What are your initial views on the way in which events are represented?

2   Are there any parts of the text that you would classify as judgements rather than reports?

3   Read through the text again, this time identifying and labelling the verbs/verbal groups as active, middle or passive voice.

4   Are there any agentless passives?

5   Suggest reasons for the use of these as well as any examples of long passives and middle voice you find.

6   Are any sources cited? If not, why not?

7   Comment on the use of technical vocabulary in the text.

8   Comment on the use of plural pronouns in the text.

9   Who is being included in the referential sphere of the plural first person pronoun in the nominative case and who is being excluded?

10   What is the prominent angle of representation in the text?

Text 16: The Campaign

Operations in Iraq: First reflections

Chapter 3: The campaign

3.1   By 18 March the Government and its coalition partners had concluded that the diplomatic process had been exhausted and that, unless Saddam Hussein complied with a final ultimatum, there would be no alternative to military action against the Iraqi regime. The Government secured Parliamentary approval on that day for the use of 'all means necessary' to ensure the destruction of Iraq's weapons of mass destruction.

Military campaign objectives

3.2   The overriding objective was to disarm Iraq of its weapons of mass destruction. To achieve this we would need to overcome the Iraqi security forces and remove the Iraqi regime, while denying them the ability to use weapons of mass destruction. It would also be essential to secure Iraq's key economic infrastructure from sabotage and wilful destruction by Saddam Hussein's forces, and deter wider conflict both inside Iraq and in the region. Moreover, this had to be accomplished with minimum impact on the Iraqi people, with whom we had no quarrel.

Operations begin

3.3   Although some preliminary operations against Iraqi artillery missile and air defence systems had been carried out on 19 March to reduce the threat to coalition forces in Kuwait, the military campaign proper began in the early hours of 20 March some 90 minutes after the expiry of a US ultimatum for Saddam Hussein to leave Iraq. Following intelligence about the location of senior members of the Iraqi leadership, US F-117 stealth fighters and a number of cruise missiles struck regime targets around Baghdad. Iraqi forces responded by launching five missiles into Kuwait (and more subsequently), forcing our troops and Kuwaiti civilians to don Nuclear Biological and Chemical (NBC) protective clothing as a precaution.

UK operations

3.4   The coalition plan envisaged simultaneous air and ground operations to overwhelm the regime. The land offensive began on 20 March, less than 24 hours after the first bomb was dropped. The UK planned to fight a joint campaign utilising sustainable, balanced forces that would provide commanders with the flexibility to respond to enemy actions and the emerging features of the conflict. Coalition aircraft maintained air superiority, provided Close Air Support and aerial reconnaissance and shaped the battlespace by disrupting enemy forces. Aircraft tasking was helped by embedding a network of air operation coordination and liaison cells in the land forces' chain of headquarters. Helicopters from the UK Joint Helicopter Command also provided crucial combat support to the ground operation from bases on land and at sea. UK Special Forces were active from an early stage; however, in accordance with established policy, this report does not comment on their activities.

3.5   The first objective was to seize the Al Faw peninsula and key oil installations, to secure access to the strategically important port of Umm Qasr. In an excellent example of joint and combined operations, coalition forces, led by 40 Commando (and subsequently 42 Commando) Royal Marines, launched an amphibious assault on the Al Faw peninsula, using helicopters from the Joint Helicopter Command and a variety of landing craft, supported by three Royal Navy frigates which provided Naval Fire Support. The securing of the Al Faw peninsula and the Rumaylah oilfields by UK and US forces, to whom UK NBC troops and engineer elements had been attached, was a key early success for the coalition. Although some oil wells had already been set alight, there was not the widespread sabotage that had been feared. Within 48 hours Umm Qasr had been captured and was being secured by the US 15th Marine Expeditionary Unit under the command of 3 Commando Brigade Royal Marines.

Commentary

At first glance, the text appears to be a fairly unremarkable and disinterested account of troop deployments and military objectives with little or no mention of the political ideology, violence and bloodshed usually associated with war, but it is loaded with interested lexical and grammatical choices. Even in an official military report such as this, there are examples of judgemental language expressing opinions rather than verifiable statements. For example, the possible destruction of Iraq's key economic infrastructure by Saddam Hussein's forces is described as 'wilful', helicopters from the UK Joint Helicopter Command are said to provide 'crucial combat support', and coalition forces are described as providing an 'excellent example of joint and combined operations'. The adjectives 'wilful', 'crucial' and 'excellent' express opinions that it would not be possible to verify and are therefore judgements rather than reports. There is, furthermore, only one rather vague source cited in the whole text: 'Following <u>intelligence</u> about the location of senior members of the Iraqi leadership', though even this would prove difficult to verify. The text itself, in other words, appears to claim authority.

Middle voice is used throughout the text (the non-human agent(s) in each example have been underlined):

◎   <u>US F-117 stealth fighters and a number of cruise missiles</u> struck regime targets around Baghdad.

◎   <u>Coalition aircraft</u> maintained air superiority, provided Close Air Support and aerial reconnaissance and shaped the battlespace by disrupting enemy forces.

◎   <u>Helicopters from the UK Joint Helicopter Command</u> also provided crucial combat support to the ground operation from bases on land and at sea.

It is not military personnel, but stealth fighters, cruise missiles, coalition aircraft and helicopters that are the agents of the actions of verbs such as 'strike', 'maintain', 'provide' and 'shape'. As noted in the analysis of media coverage of war, these examples of middle voice background human agency and foreground technology, thereby absolving the military of any responsibility. There are also a number of agentless passives in the text:

◎   Although some preliminary operations against Iraqi artillery missile and air defence systems <u>had been carried out</u> on 19 March to reduce the threat to coalition forces in Kuwait.

◎ The land offensive began on 20 March, less than 24 hours after the first bomb <u>was dropped</u>.

◎ The securing of the Al Faw peninsula and the Rumaylah oilfields by UK and US forces, to whom UK NBC troops and engineer elements <u>had been attached</u>.

◎ Although some oil wells <u>had</u> already <u>been set alight</u>, there was not the widespread sabotage that <u>had been feared</u>.

◎ Within 48 hours Umm Qasr <u>had been captured</u> and was being secured by the US 15th Marine Expeditionary Unit under the command of 3 Commando Brigade Royal Marines.

Once again, these allow the information in the text to be organised strategically according to the writer's objectives. They are not neutral observations, but carefully worded representations of events that have the potential to obscure or at least de-emphasise the role or involvement of the unmentioned initiating agent. Where the action is likely to be viewed negatively by the reader/listener (as in the first and second examples above), such a formulation acts to deflect criticism from those responsible.

The use of technical register and initialisms such as 'F-117', 'NBC', 'battlespace', 'tasking' and 'liaison cells' gives a false sense of accuracy and sophistication. Vague and highly evasive terms such as 'preliminary operations' and 'Fire Support' are also used in order to make the unpleasant seem more palatable.

The plural first person pronoun in the nominative case is used twice (paragraph 3.2) and the plural first person pronoun in the genitive case (adjective) is used once (paragraph 3.3). The plural third person pronoun in the accusative case is used in reference to the 'Iraqi security forces' and 'Iraqi regime', but the writer takes great pains to ensure that the 'Iraqi people' are not included in the referential sphere: 'Moreover, this had to be accomplished with minimum impact on the Iraqi people, with whom we had no quarrel.' The reader is left in no doubt that only British military personnel are being included in the referential sphere of 'we', since it is only the armed forces who would be able to 'overcome the Iraqi security forces and remove the Iraqi regime' by force. Exactly who is being included in the referential sphere of 'our', however, is more difficult to ascertain; it could be either the military leadership or British people. Either way, the lexical and grammatical choices in the text are highly manipulative and far from disinterested.

Extension

1 Write three brief judgements and three brief reports on the 'War on Terror'.

2 Exchange your judgements and reports with a partner then label your partner's work as either judgements or reports.

3 Feed back your findings to others in your group and discuss.

FURTHER READING

Dawes, J. (2002) *The Language of War: Literature and culture in the US from the Civil War through World War II*. Cambridge, MA: Harvard University Press.

Virtual war

In Unit two: Verbal armoury, we noted that cinema is one of the ways in which the language of war has entered mainstream usage. In this unit, we will consider another: video games. Video games have overtaken films as the world's most successful entertainment medium. In the *Australian Entertainment and Media Outlook Report* (2003), PricewaterhouseCoopers estimated the 2002 global market for interactive video game software to be worth $40.9 billion, surpassing the total global film box office takings of $39.6 billion. As with films, the US dominates both production and distribution. US video games find their way, either officially or through large-scale bootlegging, to people all over the world. Public debate usually focuses on the level of violence, but recently many of these games have acquired a strong political message too. In this unit, we will unpack the political message of the language of war games using the analytical techniques discussed in previous chapters. This will enable you to consolidate the knowledge that you have acquired.

There are many different genres of video game on the market today. From platform games to flight simulators, each of these genres has created a niche market within the huge worldwide population of computer gamers. One of the fastest growing genres is the 'first-person shoot-'em-up'. First-person shoot-'em-ups (also known as 'first-person shooters' or FPSs) are fast-paced three-dimensional video games where the player's on-screen view of the game world simulates that of the character. Most first-person shoot-'em-ups place the player behind some sort of firearm with the player's 'hand' holding the weapon. This first-person perspective is meant to give the player a vivid sense of what it is like to engage in armed combat.

Activity

Text 17: You Don't Play, You Volunteer is from the packaging for the Xbox™ first-person shoot-'em-up *Medal of Honor: Frontline* (2002), produced by EA Games. This game is one in a series of *Medal of Honor* titles based on Second World War battles. According to the 'game info' on the EA Games website (www.moh.ea.com): 'In this installment of the smash-hit Medal of Honor series, Lt. Patterson [a US soldier] returns and must infiltrate the German frontline to steal the HO-IX flying wing, an experimental Nazi weapon so powerful it could turn the tide of World War II.'

1   Comment on the use of verbal language in the text, paying particular attention to the use of pronouns, verbs and initialisms.

2   Suggest possible reasons for lexical choice.

3   Comment on the interplay between verbal and visual language.

4   What sort of audience do you think this text was intended for?

Text 17: You Don't Play, You Volunteer

Commentary

Text 17: You Don't Play, You Volunteer contains five screenshots of the game (one of which is a split-screen multiplayer screenshot) and the use of direct verbal language is intended to complement the direct visual first-person perspective. As in Text 9: Britons, the singular second person pronoun in the nominative case is used (twice in the first sentence) to attract the attention of potential buyers/players of the game by addressing them directly. The verbs 'play' and 'volunteer', both of which have a subject (i.e. 'you'), are contrasted in order to suggest that this is more than just a game. The verbs 'storm', 'outsmart', 'sabotage', 'defeat', 'outgun', 'fight', 'master', 'penetrate', 'learn', 'engage', 'go' and 'play', on the other hand, are all in the imperative mood and do not have a subject. This is because the subject has already been established. Sentences with an imperative as their main verb typically require the person(s) addressed to carry out an action, as in recipes (see Unit two: Verbal armoury), and the author(s) of the text may be attempting to mimic the language of the parade ground, where commands are also given in the imperative mood. Verbs such as 'master' and 'penetrate', furthermore, have distinctly male connotations, so it would be reasonable to assume that the text was intended for a predominantly male audience.

Two initialisms are used in the text: SS and OSS. SS is from the German 'Schutzstaffel': Schutz (defence) + Staffel (echelon), an elite quasi-military unit of the Nazi party that served as Hitler's personal guard and as a special security force in Germany and the occupied countries during the Second World War. Although the German origin of this initialism may be obscure to most, even non-military personnel will have heard of it. It is doubtful, however, whether many will have heard of OSS (Office of Strategic Services), let alone know that it was one of the first US intelligence agencies. The purpose of its use is to make those who play the game feel as if they belong to an exclusive group.

Doom (1993), created by id Software, is often credited as the video game that defined the first-person shoot-'em-up genre. This game involves the player assuming the role of a futuristic soldier and killing a variety of zombies, cyborgs and demons. More recent games have involved the player in re-enacting historical battles (see any of the games in the *Medal of Honor* series) or assuming the role of a modern-day soldier and killing a variety of human adversaries. *Delta Force* (1998), for example, was developed and published by the US company NovaLogic, which has partnerships with 'defense contractors' such as Lockheed Martin and

Sikorsky, and is also involved in creating simulations for the US Army. In this first-person shoot-'em-up, the player is a US Special Forces soldier sent on a series of secret missions to seek and destroy 'terrorists': a collection of drug traffickers, hostage takers and revolutionaries. During gameplay, the player is told that terrorists plan attacks on US embassies and have taken hostages, but not why:

> In October of 1977, the 1st Special Forces Operational Detachment-DELTA was secretly formed to deal with the growing threat of world terrorism. At Fort Bragg, elite Delta Force operatives, recruited mainly from the 82nd Airborne, Special Forces Green Berets and US Army Rangers, rigorously train in hostage rescues, specialized reconnaissance and other counter terrorism techniques. Highly skilled in CQB (Close Quarters Battle), armed with the best equipment, and able to infiltrate as civilians, Delta Force is ready to deal with the most dangerous world threats. Due to the extremely sensitive nature of these low-visibility missions, the US Department of Defense still does not officially acknowledge the existence of Delta Force. You are the hunter. This is what you've trained for . . . what you live for . . . YOU are Delta Force.

(Note the use of the passive voice in the first sentence, the acronym 'DELTA', the initialism 'CQB' and, as in Text 17: You Don't Play, You Volunteer, the use of the singular second person pronoun in the nominative case to directly address the reader.) The player learns nothing about what has driven these people to traffick in drugs, take hostages or rebel. The emphasis, instead, is entirely on the military hardware at the player's disposal and the 'realistic' gameplay, as is evident in the following reviews of the game posted on the internet:

> In some missions you'll want to find a nice place to hide and kill. For these types of outings, you'll have two choices. First there's the M40A1 Sniper Rifle which boasts an 800m effective range and an 8x scope (you can see up the enemy's nose with this eyepiece). If you're fairly sure that you're going to be a really long way away, you may want to consider the Barrett Light .50 which has an effective range of 1500m and also has an 8x scope.
> (pc.ign.com/articles/160/160223p1.html)

> First off, let's begin with the gameplay. One of Delta Force's greatest strengths is the level of reality this game brings to the PC. Ignore the graphics and sound and other dressings; you could actually buy

this game for its gameplay alone. It is that much fun. But beware, it is extremely addictive.

(gr.bolt.com/games/pc/action/delta_force.htm)

Delta Force: Black Hawk Down (2002) is another first-person shoot-'em-up produced by NovaLogic. In this game, the player is a Delta Force soldier sent into Somalia to protect the Red Cross from attacks by gangster-style 'terrorists'. Again, the player learns nothing about the historical context of the conflict. For example, the player is not told that the US, in support of the brutal dictator Siad Barre, had been shipping weapons into Somalia for several decades in exchange for bases in the region. Nothing is said about the US withdrawal from Somalia once bases had been acquired elsewhere. The player is not told that the Red Cross was then forced to distribute food with the help of clan leaders (termed 'warlords' by the Western media), nor that the US refused to send in troops until the famine was over, against the wishes of the Red Cross. According to Lee Milligan, President of NovaLogic:

> In Operation Restore Hope [the US attack on Mogadishu in 1993] the men of Task Force ranger fought a fierce battle in what is now recognised as the war on terrorism. In *Delta Force: Black Hawk Down*, gamers will step into the shoes of US Special Operations Forces tackling some of their most dangerous missions. We dedicate this game to the men who were there, to Delta Force, Rangers, Navy SEALs and the 160th SOAR.

(Note the use of the acronyms SEAL and SOAR.) In other words, it is perfectly acceptable to kill people if the US government defines them as 'terrorists', 'warlords' or, as appears to be the current preference, 'insurgents'.

Activity

1   Rent a selection of first-person shoot-'em-up war games from your local video shop. (These can be either PC, PlayStation®, PlayStation® 2, NINTENDO GAMECUBE or Xbox™ games.)

2   Comment on the language used on-screen during gameplay, on the packaging of the game and/or in the manual provided with the game.

3   What background, if any, is given to the conflict?

4   What is the predominant angle of representation?

5   How is language used to differentiate between an 'us' and a 'them'?

6   What kinds of words are used to identify 'the other'?

7   Comment on the use of initialisms and acronyms in the description of weaponry.

8   How often is the passive voice used in the game manual and for what purpose?

(There is no commentary for this activity.)

America's Army (2002) is an online team-based tactical first-person shoot-'em-up. In many respects it resembles any other first-person shoot-'em-up but, unlike commercial games such as *Medal of Honor: Frontline, Doom, Delta Force* and *Delta Force: Black Hawk Down*, it was specifically designed by the US Army as a recruitment tool. According to Major Christopher Chambers of the US Army's Office of Economic and Manpower Analysis, however:

> *America's Army* is a communication tool designed to show players what the army is – a high-tech, exciting organization with lots to do. We know that Americans love this type of electronic entertainment. It just made sense the army communicates its story where people like to spend time. There are no embedded messages. This is simply an entertaining and informative tool to connect with America about what the Army is about.

In an internet article entitled '"America's Army" Targets Youth' (2002), Jacob Hodes and Emma Ruby-Sachs point out that US Army recruitment figures in 1999 were at their lowest for over 30 years:

> In response, Congress called for 'aggressive, innovative experiments' to find new soldiers, and the Defense Department jacked up recruitment budgets to $2.2 billion a year. Hence we have *America's Army*, one of a number of new initiatives designed to help the military reach America's youth . . . enlistment quotas have now been met for two years straight. But the goal of the revamped recruiting campaign is not just to raise short-term recruiting numbers, it also aims to ensure a steady stream of recruits in the long term. The

goal, as spelled out in testimony before the Senate Armed Services Committee, is to penetrate youth culture and get the Army into a young person's 'consideration set,' as Timothy Maude, the Army's deputy chief of personnel, put it. By reaching kids when they're young, the Pentagon hopes they will develop a level of comfort with the military that will increase their propensity to enlist later.

The game, which involves the player assuming the role of a modern-day US soldier, consists of two parts: *Soldiers: Empower Yourself*, a role-playing segment intended to instil US Army values, and *Operations: Defend Freedom*, a first-person combat simulator where players engage in virtual warfare over the internet. (When *Operations* launches, a hyper-link in the main menu takes the player directly to www.goarmy.com/flindex.jsp, a key US Army recruitment website.) A team at the US Naval Postgraduate School's Modeling, Virtual Environment and Simulation Institute spent three years and over $5 million ensuring that the game was as accurate as possible. Despite this attention to technical detail, the violence is largely sanitised: there are no sound effects and very little blood is shed when players are shot.

Activity

Text 18: Special Forces Hospital is from the missions 'game intel' section of the *America's Army* website (www.americasarmy.com/intel/map_sfhospital.php). All gamers are required to read this intelligence before playing the 'SF Hospital' mission.

1   Comment on the field, mode and tenor of the text.

2   What function does the use of technical register serve?

3   In what way does the use of language in the text symbolise member-ship of a particular group?

4   Is any degree of prior shared knowledge assumed? If so, who is being included and who is being excluded?

Text 18: Special Forces Hospital

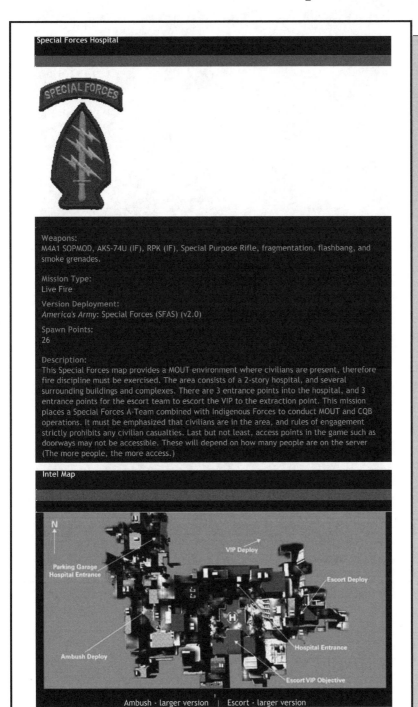

Special Forces Hospital

Weapons:
M4A1 SOPMOD, AKS-74U (IF), RPK (IF), Special Purpose Rifle, fragmentation, flashbang, and smoke grenades.

Mission Type:
Live Fire

Version Deployment:
America's Army: Special Forces (SFAS) (v2.0)

Spawn Points:
26

Description:
This Special Forces map provides a MOUT environment where civilians are present, therefore fire discipline must be exercised. The area consists of a 2-story hospital, and several surrounding buildings and complexes. There are 3 entrance points into the hospital, and 3 entrance points for the escort team to escort the VIP to the extraction point. This mission places a Special Forces A-Team combined with Indigenous Forces to conduct MOUT and CQB operations. It must be emphasized that civilians are in the area, and rules of engagement strictly prohibits any civilian casualties. Last but not least, access points in the game such as doorways may not be accessible. These will depend on how many people are on the server (The more people, the more access.)

Intel Map

Parking Garage
Hospital Entrance

VIP Deploy

Escort Deploy

Hospital Entrance

Ambush Deploy

Escort VIP Objective

Ambush - larger version | Escort - larger version

Escort Briefing

Situation:
Following an ambush by enemy forces, a wounded Resistance leader escaped to a neutral hospital for treatment of his wounds. The leader is a critical member of the Resistance government within Unconventional Warfare Area of Operations (UWAO) JAZZ.

Rules of Engagement:
Standard ROE is in effect. Minimize harm to local population. Be especially careful to protect the hospital workers and hospital facilities during this operation.

Mission:
ODA 212 assaults Objective KUHIO, vicinity ZZ 031441, commencing 14 0700 MAR 04, to exfiltrate the friendly Resistance leader in order to maintain continuity of Resistance leadership in UWAO JAZZ..

Friendly:
Enemy forces, supported by foreign advisors, are believed to have launched a snatch-team to seize the Resistance leader and any documents in his possession.

Troops:
Split Team "Alpha" 212 and Resistance Fire Team.

Terrain:
The hospital is located in a no-man's land between friendly and enemy forces operating within the city. Many civilians are operating in the hospital and scattered throughout the area.

Assault Briefing

Situation:
A wounded enemy courier has been abandoned at a neutral hospital following the hasty retreat of enemy forces. The courier is believed to be in possession of military plans for future offensive operations in Unconventional Warfare Area of Operations (UWAO) JAZZ.

Rules of Engagement:
Standard ROE is in effect. Minimize harm to the local population. Be especially careful to protect the hospital workers and hospital facilities during this operation.

Mission:
ODA 211 assaults Objective KUHIO, vicinity ZZ 031441, commencing 14 0700 MAR 04, to seize military documents in order to analyze and counter future enemy offensive operations.

Enemy:
Enemy forces, supported by foreign advisors, are believed to have launched a small team to rescue the wounded courier.

Friendly:
Split Team "Alpha" 211 and Resistance Fire Team.

Terrain:
The hospital is located in a no-man's land between friendly and enemy forces operating within the city. Many civilians are operating in the hospital and scattered throughout the area.

(There is no commentary for this activity.)

There are four combat missions in *America's Army Operations*: defend an Alaskan oil pipeline against 'terrorist saboteurs', safeguard an 'enemy prisoner of war', raid a 'terrorist training camp' and cross a bridge held by 'enemy forces'. All missions follow the same script: we (i.e. the US Army) are good and they (i.e. the other) are bad. Most of the combat missions explicitly feature 'terrorists' as the villains. Other missions are less specific, referring only to 'insurgent forces' or 'enemies'. According to Hodes and Ruby-Sachs (2002):

> The first level we played, 'Insurgent Camp,' is modeled after an early campaign of the war in Afghanistan. The setting is described as 'high desert with rolling sand dunes and wadis' (Arabic for valley), and the mission is to make a pre-emptive raid on a terrorist training camp. We failed miserably at our objective (those like us who have no video-game experience tend to be gunned down in short order). Luckily, the game provides a corpse view, and from there we watched the action. As quiet stretches were punctuated by bursts of gunfire, conversation went back and forth between our teammates, all participating in the same virtual battle from their homes, offices or dorm rooms. 'Take that, you dirty Arabs,' one player radioed after a successful strike. This sparked a debate among fellow players regarding whether Afghans are actually Arab. The squadron eventually concluded that it doesn't really matter, since 'ragheads are ragheads.'

Although it is stated in the *America's Army* 'Rules of Engagement' that 'Derogatory language or slander involving race, gender, sexual preference, religion or creed will not be tolerated', terms with negative connotations such as 'dirty Arab' and 'raghead' are obviously overlooked by the game's moderators. Players are thus conditioned to accept pro-US Manichaeanism (see Unit three: Us and them), and the game not only legitimises war as the natural way of solving inter-group conflict, but also validates the US 'war on terror'. As Hodes and Ruby-Sachs (2002) put it, 'Players learn, in this army, that war is fun.'

Activity

1   Can you suggest any reasons why the Pentagon, in the words of US Army spokesman Paul Boyce, should be 'very careful on the blood thing' when developing *America's Army*?

89

2   Comment on US Major Christopher Chambers' assertion that *America's Army* contains 'no embedded messages'.

3   In Unit one: Fighting talk, it was suggested that the naturalisation of language better suited to war adversely affects the way we interact with others. What effect, if any, do you think the verbal and visual language of first person shoot-'em-ups has on computer gamers?

(There is no commentary for this activity.)

Extension

1   Research the origins and history of chess, paying particular attention to terminology such as 'checkmate'. Although the origins of 'checkmate' are obscure, many chess terms are now in common use. Does the popularity of confrontational games such as chess limit our ability to live our lives peacefully?

2   Analyse the language used to promote strategy board games such as Risk, Battleships, Stratego, Attack!, Axis & Allies, Bosworth, Wings of War, Memoir '44, Diplomacy, World in Flames and Battle Cry.

answers and commentaries

Unit one (Text 2: The Battle for Beauty), p. 6

The dominant metaphor is clearly that of war. There are a number of conceptual metaphors supporting the central structural metaphor that to remain beautiful is a constant all-out war against the ageing process. The article is not only entitled 'The *battle* for beauty', but in the subtitle 'Heat from radio frequencies' is described as 'the latest *weapon* against aging skin'. The procedure is again referred to as 'the latest *weapon* in age-defying' in the second paragraph, and this analogy is extended throughout the article. In the caption beneath the photograph, for example, Thermage is described as a procedure that 'uses radio frequency to *target* deep layers of the skin', and in the ninth paragraph we are informed that: 'Thermage is *aimed* at people 35–55.' A cosmetic surgeon quoted in the fifth paragraph describes the technique as 'a missing *weapon* in the *arsenal* of anti-aging procedures'. In the same paragraph, the metaphorical use of the **noun phrase** 'pre-emptive strike', a reference to the way in which military objectives are targeted before they are able to launch an effective attack, implies that the ageing process is best tackled before physical signs of age begin to show.

Unit two, p. 27

AO:	area of operations
AWACS:	airborne warning and control system
C&C:	command and control
DADCAP:	dawn and dusk combat air patrol
DEFCON:	defence readiness conditions
DMZ:	demilitarised zone
E&E:	escape and evasion
EPW:	enemy prisoner of war
ERW:	enhanced radiation weapon
FIBUA:	fighting in built-up areas
GI:	general issue
GSW:	gunshot wound
HARM:	high-speed anti-radiation missile
HQ:	headquarters

HVT: high-value target
ICBM: intercontinental ballistic missile
KIA: killed in action
LGB: laser guided bomb
LOCAP: low combat air patrol
LP: listening post
LZ: landing zone
MAD: mutually assured destruction
MBT: main battle tank
MFC: mortar fire controller
MIA: missing in action
MIRV: multiple independently targetable re-entry vehicle
MOAB: massive ordnance air blast
MOPP: mission-oriented protective posture
MOUT: military operations on urbanised terrain
MP: military police
PDF: principal direction of fire
POW: prisoner of war
PTSD: post-traumatic stress disorder
RFA: royal fleet auxiliary
RPG: rocket-propelled grenade
R&R: rest and recreation
SAM: surface-to-air missile
SLBM: submarine-launched ballistic missile
SNAFU: situation normal, all fucked up
SSE: sensitive site exploitation
SSK: single shot to kill
TLAM: tactical land attack missile
TPFDL: time-phased forces deployment list
TWS: tactical weapon system
UXB: unexploded bomb
WIA: wounded in action
WP: white phosphorus

War films, war literature and war games have helped to popularise acronyms and initialisms such as DEFCON , GI , HQ , POW and UXB, but most would not be understood by non-military personnel. The use of acronyms and initialisms such as these plays a three-fold role. First, and perhaps most importantly for the user, the use of these terms signals group membership, which in turn strengthens social bonds with those in the same group. Second, they exclude all non-military personnel. Third, and perhaps most significantly, terms such as these seek to distance us further from the full horror of what they describe.

Unit three, p. 38–9

Declassified documents posted on the internet by the National Security Archive (2003) show the British Embassy in Baghdad recommending Saddam Hussein to London in 1969 as a 'presentable young man' with an 'engaging smile', 'with whom, if only one could see more of him, it would be possible to do business'. All of this is in stark contrast to more recent accounts of Saddam Hussein, which portray him as 'cruel', 'brutal', 'barbaric' and 'insane' – a standard tactic used in propaganda. In an article published in *The Guardian* (4 October 2001), Philip Knightley points out:

> The way wars are reported in the western media follows a depressingly predictable pattern: stage one, the crisis; stage two, the demonisation of the enemy's leader [comparing the leader with Hitler is a good start because of the instant images that Hitler's name provokes]; stage three, the demonisation of the enemy as individuals; and stage four, atrocities.

The purpose of such demonisation is ultimately to make war sound more acceptable and justify military action.

You may have noticed that the term 'spider hole' was frequently used in both the US and British media to describe the place where Saddam Hussein was hiding when he was captured. On the American CNN, CBC and Fox websites, furthermore, news of Saddam Hussein's capture was broken with the headline: 'Saddam "caught like a rat" in a hole.' (The quote, 'He was in the bottom of a hole with no way to fight back. He was caught like a rat', is attributed in all three cases to US Major General Raymond Odierno.) As in Wilson's (1901) description of Boer shelters as 'lairs', these far from insignificant lexical choices serve the dual purpose of dehumanising Saddam Hussein and thereby absolving the American and British forces in Iraq of any wrongdoing.

Unit four (Text 8: Airdrop Propaganda Leaflet), p. 50

This leaflet was airdropped over Iraqi military positions in Kuwait and was intended to be read by Iraqi soldiers. The cartoon depicts Saddam Hussein cutting off his own head with a sword and is deceptively simple in appearance, as if its only purpose is to induce laughter at Saddam Hussein's expense. It effectively conveys how Iraq might suffer because of Saddam

Hussein's reckless and aggressive actions. It also employs the visual equivalent of the type of verbal name-calling discussed in Unit three: Us and them. Saddam Hussein is not only depicted as an idiot capable of accidentally beheading himself, but his paunch, poor physique, big head, facial expression, lack of clothing (note, however, the epaulets) and gestures are all intended to make him look as ridiculous as possible. The main propagandistic message of the leaflet appears to be that Saddam Hussein is an incompetent fool unworthy of military leadership: someone more concerned with his own sense of self-importance than with the Iraqi people.

Shadows at Saddam Hussein's feet are cleverly used to show **deictic** expressions of time. (Note: for a full explanation of deixis, see Unit three of the core book in the series, *Working with Texts*.) In the first cartoon the shadows are to Saddam Hussein's left. In the second cartoon the shadow is to his right, and in the third it appears to be directly beneath him. This indicates the passage of time and implies that this is not the first occasion that Saddam Hussein has been an incompetent fool. The use of English rather than Arabic gives the impression that the leaflet was primarily intended to be distributed among the US and other English-speaking forces and that they were airdropped over Iraqi positions by mistake. The US Army Department of Psychological Warfare designed the leaflet to anger rather than amuse in the hope that Iraqi soldiers picking it up and reading it would share their indignation with others and thus help circulate it further afield. The message attempts to manipulate with emotion and does so rather effectively.

Unit 5 (Texts 13: *Salem Gazette* and 14: *London Gazette*), pp. 67–8

The two texts differ a great deal in their accounts of the conflict at Lexington and include both judgements and reports. Distinguishing between judgements and reports is far from simple, but when viewing, reading or listening to war coverage it is a vital skill – one that can prevent viewers, readers and listeners falling prey to propaganda. The *Salem Gazette* writes of 'the savage barbarity exercised upon the bodies of our unfortunate brethren'. The *London Gazette* states that the Americans 'went off in great confusion' and also writes about 'the cruelty and barbarity of the rebels'. 'Savage', 'unfortunate', 'great confusion', 'cruelty' and, of course, 'barbarity' (see Unit three: Us and them) express opinions and are therefore not reports.

According to the *Salem Gazette*, the first shots were fired by 'one or two officers' of the British armed forces, whereas the *London Gazette* states that 'several guns were fired upon the King's Troops'. Both are reports, since they exclude judgemental language and could be verified as either true or not true, though both include generalities (i.e. 'one or two' and 'several').

However, both reports cannot be true. Determining which one is true would require further investigation that might or might not produce a definitive answer. It is arguable, furthermore, whether there is ever any single, absolute 'fact' or 'truth' waiting to be discovered and reported upon. Different reports can lead to very different interpretations of the same event, and, in any kind of report, the presenter, writer or broadcaster will have to select what to omit, what to report, and which sources to consult. In doing so, they will inevitably render their version of events a subjective rather than objective representation of events.

references

Bell, A. (1991) *The Language of News Media*. Oxford: Blackwell.

Biber, D., Johansson, S. and Leech, G. *et al.* (1999) *The Longman Grammar of Spoken and Written English*. London: Longman.

Cartwright, D. (1963) 'Some principles of mass persuasion' in G. Maletzke *Psychologie der Massenkommunikation*. Hamburg: Verlag Hans Bredow-Institut.

Fairclough, N. (1995). *Critical Discourse Analysis: The critical study of language*. London: Longman.

Ford, Peter (2001) 'Europe cringes at Bush "Crusade" against terrorists', *Christian Science Monitor*, 19 September.

Goodman, S. and Graddol, D. (1996) *Redesigning English: New texts, new identities*. London: Routledge.

Hodes, J. and Ruby-Sachs, E. (2002) '"America's Army" Targets Youth', www.thenation.com/doc/20020902/hodes20020823

Lakoff, G. (2003) *Metaphors We Live By*. Chicago, IL: University of Chicago Press.

Luskin, J. (1972) *Lippmann, Liberty and the Press*. Tuscaloosa, AL: The University of Alabama Press.

Lutz, W. (1987) *Doublespeak: from 'revenue enhancement' to 'terminal living': How government, business, advertisers, and others use language to deceive you*. New York: Harper & Row.

Lutz, W. (1994) 'Double speak' in R. Greenberg and J. Comprone *Contexts and Communities: Rhetorical approaches to reading and writing*. New York: Macmillan.

Lutz, W. (1996) *The New Doublespeak: Why no one knows what anyone's saying anymore*. New York: HarperCollins.

Lutz, W. (1999) *Doublespeak Defined: Cut through the bull**** and get the point*. New York: HarperResource.

Montgomery, M. (1995) *An Introduction to Language and Society*. London: Routledge.

Mühlhäusler, P. and Harré, R. (1990) *Pronouns and People: The linguistic construction of social and personal identity*. Oxford: Blackwell.

Nash, W. (1990) *Language in Popular Fiction*. London: Routledge.

Orwell, G. (1946) 'Politics and the English Language', *Horizon* (No. 36, April 1946).

Orwell, G. (1949) *1984*. London: Secker & Warburg.

Said, E. (1995) *Orientalism*. London: Penguin.

Saunders, D. (1999) *Twentieth Century Advertising*. London: Carlton Books.

Schäffner, C. and Wenden, A. (1999) *Language and Peace*. Amsterdam: Harwood Academic Press.

Seldes, G. (1929) *You Can't Print That! The truth behind the news*. Garden City, NY: Garden City.

Tannen, D. (1998) *The Argument Culture*. New York: Random House.

Trudgill, P. (1999) 'Standard English: What it isn't' in T. Bex and R. Watts *Standard English: The widening debate*. London: Routledge.

Truss, L. (2003) *Eats, Shoots and Leaves*. London: Profile.

Wilson, H. (1901) *With the Flag to Pretoria*. London: Harmsworth Brothers.

index of terms

accent 16
A peculiarity of pronunciation that indicates a person's regional and/or social origins.

accusative 30
A noun or pronoun that is the direct **object** of a **clause** is in the accusative case.

acronym 27
A word composed of the initial letters of the name of something, usually an organisation and normally pronounced as a whole word. For example, 'NATO' (North Atlantic Treaty Organization) is an acronym.

active voice 57
In the active voice, the **subject** of a **clause** is the **agent** of an action. For example, 'Shakespeare wrote Hamlet'; 'He stole my TV.' (See also **middle voice; passive voice.**)

adjective 18
Adjectives modify **nouns, noun phrases** or **pronouns** (the *beautiful* painting) and can themselves be modified by **adverbs** (underlined) (the <u>extremely</u> *competitive* team). Adjectives can have morphemes added to them to express degrees of comparison (the *oldest* pupil in the school) and they can also stand alone to describe the qualities and features of a noun (the house was very *old* and *spooky*).

adjunct 58
Adjuncts supply additional details to the information supplied by **subjects, verbs** and **objects** in a **clause**. They typically take the form of prepositional phrases (in a minute) or **adverbs** (quickly).

adverb 99
Adverbs describe and are attached to **verbs** (he ran *quickly*). Adverbs may also modify **adjectives** or other adverbs.

agent 57
The agent of a **clause** is the person or thing performing the action. In both of the following sentences, for example, 'John' is the agent: 'John wrote the letter'; 'The letter was written by John.'

agentless passive 59
An agentless passive, also known as a short passive, is where the **agent** responsible for an action is not included. For example, 'The demonstrators were shot' is a short or agentless passive, whereas 'The demonstrators were shot by the police' is a long passive that includes the agents responsible for the action (i.e. the police).

analogy 2
A comparison drawn in order to show a similarity between two things that are otherwise dissimilar.

angle of representation 59
The particular way of viewing the world that is conveyed by the grammatical relations in a particular text.

antonym 25
One of two words or other expressions that have opposite meanings. For example, 'good' and 'bad' are antonyms.

case 30
A term used for a set of forms for a **noun**, **pronoun** or **adjective**.

clause 18
A structural unit that is part of a **sentence** either as a main clause, which can stand alone and be equivalent to a sentence, or as a **subordinate** or dependent clause. For example, 'The owner, who lives abroad, has written to all the neighbours' consists of a main clause, 'The owner . . . has written to all the neighbours', and a subordinate clause, 'who lives abroad'.

cliché 2
A word or phrase that has become trite and commonplace through overuse.

cognitive structure 43
A mental map, scheme or networked concept used to understand, remember and respond to physical experiences.

collective noun 10
A **noun** used to refer to a group of people, animals or things, and occurring in the **singular** with a singular or plural **verb**. For example, 'army', 'crowd', 'herd', 'flock', 'batch' and 'flotilla' are collective nouns.

colloquialism 18
A term used to refer to language that shows characteristics of informal speech.

conceptual metaphor 10
A **metaphor** that supports and strengthens a central or **structural metaphor**. For example, 'His criticisms were right on target', is a conceptual metaphor supporting the structural metaphor that argument is war.

conjunction 18
A general term that describes words linking **sentences** and **clauses** together, indicating temporal, spatial, logical and causal relationships. Words such as 'and', 'but', 'therefore' and 'because' are conjunctions. Conjunctions are also termed 'connectives'.

connotation 25
The connotations of a word are the associations it creates. For example, the connotations of December, mainly within British and North American culture, would be of 'cold', 'dark nights' and 'Christmas parties'. Connotations are often either individual or cultural.

dead metaphor 2
A **metaphor** that has lost its initial potency due to over-exposure.

deictic 94
Deictics are words or images that point backwards, forwards and extratextually. For example, in the sentence, 'I'm going to get some wine from that shop over there', the main deictic words are 'that' and 'there'.

denotation 47
The literal, dictionary definition of a word.

dialect 16
Peculiarities of pronunciation, vocabulary and grammar that indicate a person's regional and/or social origins.

direct address 52
Direct address is an expression in which the person being spoken to is identified. For example, 'I've no idea, Sue' is a form of direct address identifying Sue as the addressee.

dysphemism 18
A 'strong' term, often of disapproval – the opposite of **euphemism**. For example, 'kick the bucket' is a dysphemism because it can be used in place of relatively neutral terms such as 'die', 'expire' or 'perish'.

etymology 11
The etymology of a word is its origin and history, including changes in its form and meaning.

euphemism 23
A mild or evasive term for something that is taboo, negative, offensive or too direct – the opposite of **dysphemism**. For example, the Nazis used the euphemism 'Endlosung' (Final Solution) to refer to the mass murder of Jews, Gypsies, homosexuals and others during the Second World War.

field 16
The subject matter of a text.

gender 30
The three genders of English **pronouns** are masculine (he/him/his/himself), feminine (she/her/hers/herself) and neuter (it/it/its/itself).

genitive 30
The possessive forms of nouns (*Connie's* hair) or pronouns (*her* hair) are in the genitive case.

genre 8
Another word for 'text type'. Examples of genre are narrative, report, argument, poetry and drama.

imperative mood 16
The imperative is the mood of a **verb** that gives commands. The **subject** is generally omitted in imperatives. For example, 'Stop!'

initialism 18
A feature of words in which whole words are abbreviated to initial letters. For example, 'BBC' (British Broadcasting Corporation) is an initialism.

lexeme 101
A unit in the **lexicon** or vocabulary of a language. Lexeme or 'lexical item' is sometimes used in order to avoid difficulties of referring to 'words'. For example, the abstract lexeme 'walk' underlies all the separate instances: 'walks', 'walked', 'walking'.

lexicon 28
A term for the vocabulary of a language or sub language, consisting of its stock of **lexemes**.

metaphor 1
A word or phrase that establishes a comparison or **analogy** between one object or idea and another. For example, 'I *demolished* his argument' contains a comparison between argument and war, and also underlines the idea that arguments can be constructed like buildings.

middle voice 57
In the middle voice, the human **agent** of an action is omitted. For example, 'The pot roast simmered on the hob', 'The Police car collided with another vehicle'. (See also **active voice; passive voice**.)

mode 16
The means adopted for communication. For example, speech and writing are modes of communication, as are body language and smoke signals.

nominalisation 63
Nominalisation occurs when a **noun** is formed from a word belonging from another word class. For example, in the sentence 'The charity walk raised money for Cancer Research', the noun 'walk' has been formed from the **verb** 'to walk'.

nominative 30
A noun or pronoun that is the **subject** of a **clause** is in the nominative case.

noun 25
Nouns are a major class of words that are regularly inflected or otherwise marked to show **plurals** (ship/ships, mouse/mice, child/children) and to indicate possession (the *dog's* lead).

noun phrase 30
A group of words that describe a **noun**.

object 57
A noun or pronoun that is at the receiving end of a **verb**. For example, 'I hit him.'

passive voice 57
In the passive voice, the **subject** of a **clause** is affected by an action. For example, 'Hamlet was written by Shakespeare'; 'My TV was stolen.' (See also **active voice; middle voice**.)

pejorative 42
A term used to refer to a word or phrase that has a negative meaning. For example, the word 'spinster' has a basic meaning of unmarried woman but has acquired pejorative **connotations**.

person 30
First person **pronouns** are the speaker(s) or writer(s) together with any others included in the **plural** (I/me/we/us); second person pronouns are the addressee(s) and possibly others in the plural (you); and third person pronouns are others being referred to (she/her/he/him/it/it/they/them). The third person **singular** of the present **tense** also has a distinct form (he *walks*, she *walks*, it *walks*).

plural 30
A term contrasting with **singular** in the number system of a language and referring to more than one person or thing.

pronominal system 31
A term used for the system of **pronouns** in a language.

pronoun 25
Pronouns are used instead of **nouns** to refer to people or things without naming them.

register 16
A variety of language defined according to social use, such as scientific, academic, legal, religious and military language.

rhetorical device 31
A linguistic technique used to persuade rather than provide reasons or evidence.

sense 1
The meaning of a word.

sentence 18
A difficult term to define because the structure of sentences differs according to whether spoken or written language is used. Traditionally, a sentence has a **subject** and a main **verb**, though in literary texts a sentence can be a single word; in spoken English, however, structures such as 'over here', 'if you like' and 'perhaps' can constitute a sentence.

simile 1
A figure of speech in which an unrealistic comparison is made using 'like' or 'as'. For example, 'like a bull in a china shop' (said of a clumsy person) is a simile.

singular 30
A term contrasting with **plural** in the number system of a language and referring to one person or thing.

slang 18
Peculiarities of vocabulary and grammar that, unlike **accent** and **dialect**, are not geographically restricted.

structural metaphor 13
A central as opposed to supporting or **conceptual metaphor**. For example, 'She was *besieged* by suitors' is a conceptual metaphor supporting the structural metaphor that love is war.

subject 18
The subject of a sentence is normally the **noun**, **noun phrase** or **pronoun** that appears before the **verb** in statements and after the first verb in questions. For example, '*I* shouted at him' and 'Are *the children on the bus* coming to the cinema?'

subordinate clause 18
A clause that normally cannot function on its own as a **sentence**.

superlative 66
The superlative is the form of an **adjective** or **adverb** that expresses the highest or a very high degree of the quality of what is being described. For example, in the **sentence** 'Everest is the highest mountain in the world', the word 'highest' is a superlative adjective describing the **noun** 'mountain'. In the sentence: 'Of all the runners, Kelly Holmes ran the fastest', the word 'fastest' is a superlative adverb describing the **verb** 'ran'.

synonym 42
One of two words or other expressions that have the same meanings. For example, 'cheap' and 'inexpensive' are synonyms.

tenor 16
Tenor refers to the kind of social relationship enacted in or by a text and is affected by politeness, degrees of formality and the statuses of participants.

tense 58
Tense is a very important grammatical category and is mainly associated with the **verb** in a **sentence**. English has two primary tenses, the present tense and the past tense.

transitive verb 57
Transitive verbs, such as 'kick' and 'spill', require an **object**: 'He kicked the ball'; 'You spilt my drink.' Transitive verbs without an object would be considered incomplete or ungrammatical: 'He kicked'; 'You spilt.' Intransitive verbs, such as 'arrive' and 'fall', do not require a direct object: 'They have arrived'; 'He fell.'

verb 6
A verb is a major category of grammar. Verbs can be either main

verbs or auxiliary verbs. For example, in the **sentence** 'I do intend to go to the match', 'intend' is a main verb and 'do' is an auxiliary verb. Auxiliary verbs cannot normally stand on their own, whereas main verbs can: 'I intend to go to the match.' Verbs can also have other forms. Here, for example, 'to go' is the infinitive form of the verb 'go'. Verbs can be inflected to show tense. For example, 'She works hard' (present tense); 'She worked hard' (past tense). They can also form present and past participles: 'He is working' (present participle); 'He has worked' (past participle). Participles can be used as modifiers: 'The working day'; 'A worked example.' A progressive form of the verb indicates an action that is continuous. For example, 'I was walking home' is a past progressive form of the verb 'walk'.

Related titles from Routledge

War of Words

Sandra Silberstein

'This is vital reading today. At a time when hysteria is bubbling below the surface, Sandra Silberstein is cool, analytical, highly readable – and sane.'

Simon Hoggart, *The Guardian*

In a media age, wars are waged not only with bombs and planes but also with video and sound bites. *War of Words* is an incisive report from the linguistic battlefields, probing the tales told on and since 9/11 to show how Americans created consensus in the face of terror. Capturing the campaigns for America's hearts, minds, wallets and votes, Silberstein traces the key cultural conflicts and motifs that have surfaced since 9/11, including:

- attacks on critical intellectuals for their perceived 'blame America first' attitude
- the symbiotic relationship between terrorists and the media and the use of news as 'entertainment'
- the commercialisation of 9/11
- representations of Al Qaeda, the Taliban and Iraq and the justification of military action

A perceptive and disturbing account, *War of Words* reveals the role of the media in manufacturing events and illuminates the shifting sands of American collective identity in the post 9/11 world.

Hb: 0–415–29047–3
Pb: 0–415–33624–4

Available at all good bookshops
For ordering and further information please visit:
www.routledge.com